SPEC
Di

UNDERWATER PHOTOGRAPHY

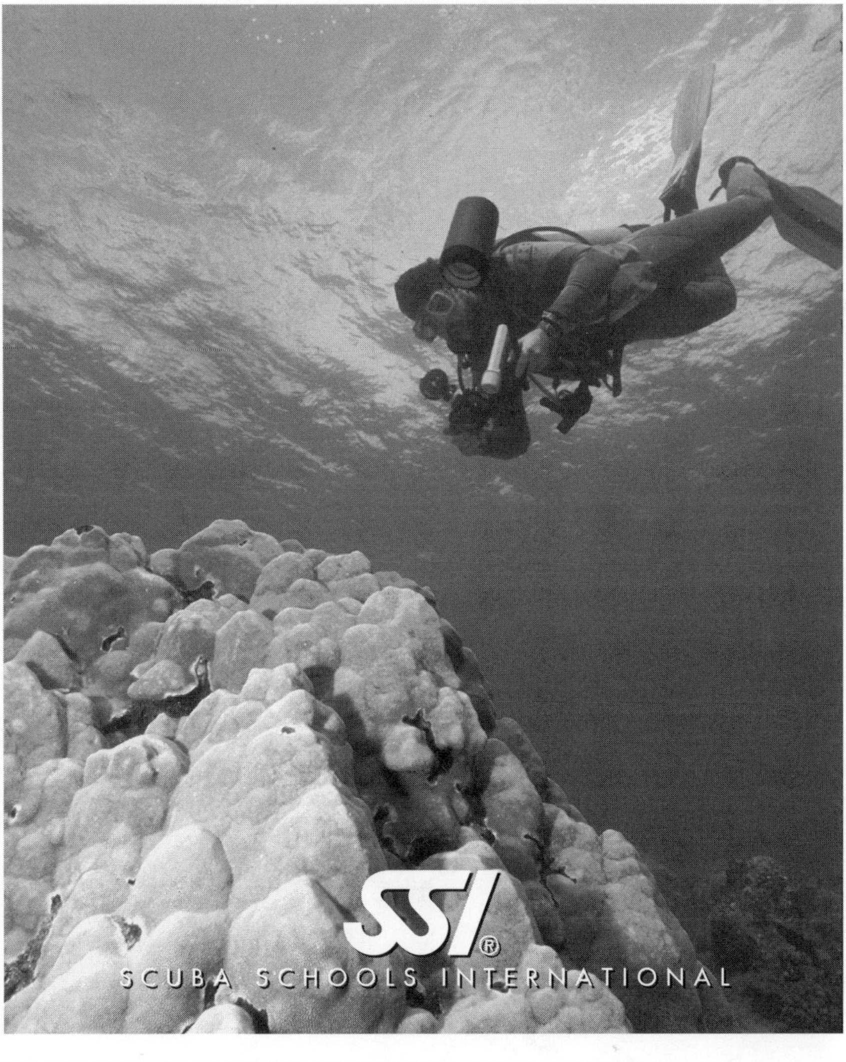

DISCLAIMER:

The information contained in the SSI training materials is intended to give an individual enrolled in a training course a broad perspective of the diving activity. There are many recommendations and suggestions regarding the use of standard and specialized equipment for the activity. Not all of the equipment discussed in the training material can, or will, be used in this activity. The choice of equipment and techniques used in the course is determined by the location of the activity, the environmental conditions and other factors.

A choice of equipment and techniques cannot be made until the dive site is surveyed immediately prior to the dive. Based on the dive site, the decision should be made regarding which equipment and techniques shall be used. The decision is that of the dive leader and the individual enrolled in the training course.

The intent of all SSI training materials is to give individuals as much information as possible in order for individuals to make their own decisions regarding the diving activity, what equipment should be used and what specific techniques may be needed. The ultimate decision on when and how to dive is that of the individual diver.

ISBN: 1-880229-26-9

First Edition
First Printing, 1/95

Printed in the USA.

SCUBA SCHOOLS INTERNATIONAL
2619 Canton Court • Fort Collins, CO 80525-4498
(303) 482-0883 • Fax (303) 482-6157

CONTENTS

Foreword . . . . **i**

Chapter 1: Getting Started **1**

Chapter 2: Selecting the Right Equipment & Film **23**

Chapter 3: Caring For Your Camera. **45**

Chapter 4: Shooting Under Water **73**

Chapter 5: Building On Your Basic Skills **95**

REORDER #2501PH

ACKNOWLEDGMENTS

Editor in Chief	**Laurie Clark Humpal**
Writer & Photographer	**Harry Averill**
Art Director	**David M. Pratt**
Graphic Designer	**Betsy Musso**
Technical Editors	**Bob Clark** **John Wall** **Bruce Hootman** **Richard Gallagher** **Dave Farrar** **Linda Nelson** **Bud Uren** **Chuck Nicklin**
Manufacturer Support	**Gale Livers** IKELITE **Joseph Gallen** SEA & SEA/GMI PHOTOGRAPHIC **Frank Fennell** NIKON, INC. **Chet Tussey** TUSSEY UNDERWATER SYSTEM
Proofing Editor	**Linda J. Clark**

Special Thanks To:

Lahaina Divers for use of their boats and facilities.

The Millbrook Quarry in Haymarket, VIrginia.

The crew of the Rampage in Riviera Beach, Florida.

And to Stephanie Rose.

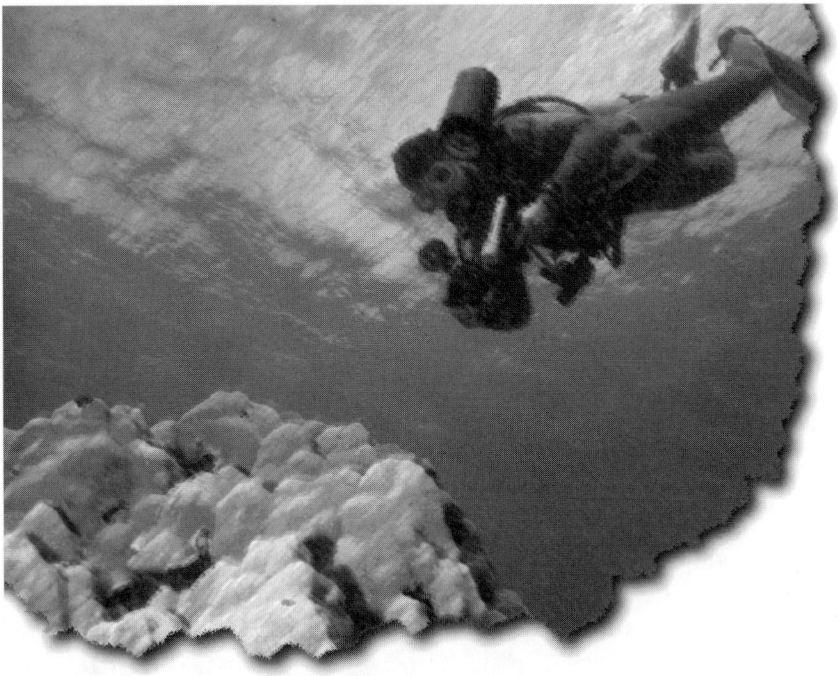

FOREWORD

WHY SPECIALTY TRAINING? The answer to "why specialty training?" is quite simple. An entry level course provides you with the motor skills, equipment knowledge, and minimum open water experience needed to be considered a safe diver. However, an Open Water Diver Course does not a specialist make.

Specialty training has two primary objectives: To prepare you for new diving situations, and to improve your level of skill. The SSI Specialty Diver Program provides an excellent introduction to a variety of different diving subjects such as Deep Diving, Boat Diving, Night Diving/Limited Visibility, and many others. These courses are designed to enhance both the enjoyment and safety of each new situation. Specialty training also develops your current level of skill to a much higher level.

Most importantly, courses such as *Underwater Photography* open up new doors and avenues of excitement for the diver. Photography provides an additional challenge for the diver while helping to develop skills such as buoyancy control.

Not every specialty is appropriate to every diver or diving level. Some specialties may not be available in your area, but can be enjoyed when traveling. Every specialty, however, can open new vistas for the diver who wishes to explore all the adventures scuba diving can provide!

> THE SSI SPECIALTY DIVER PROGRAM OFFERS THE OPPORTUNITY TO ACCELERATE THE LEARNING PROCESS THAT COULD OTHERWISE BE GAINED ONLY THROUGH TIME-CONSUMING EXPERIENCE.

The SSI Specialty Diver Program offers the opportunity, through continuing education, to accelerate the learning process that otherwise could only be gained through significant, time-consuming experience. You can quickly prepare yourself to be comfortable in whatever diving situations apply to you personally.

Here is a simple, inexpensive way to gain knowledge, experience, safety and recognition, in classes tailored to your specific interests!

Getting Started

1

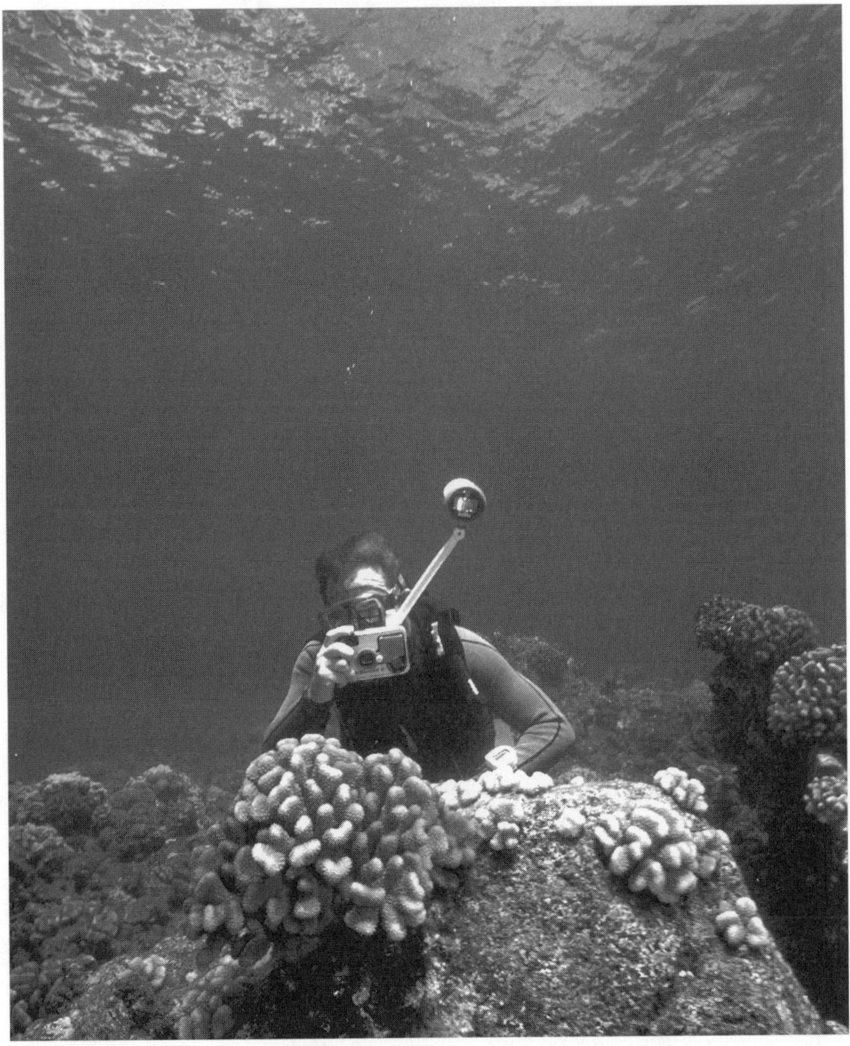

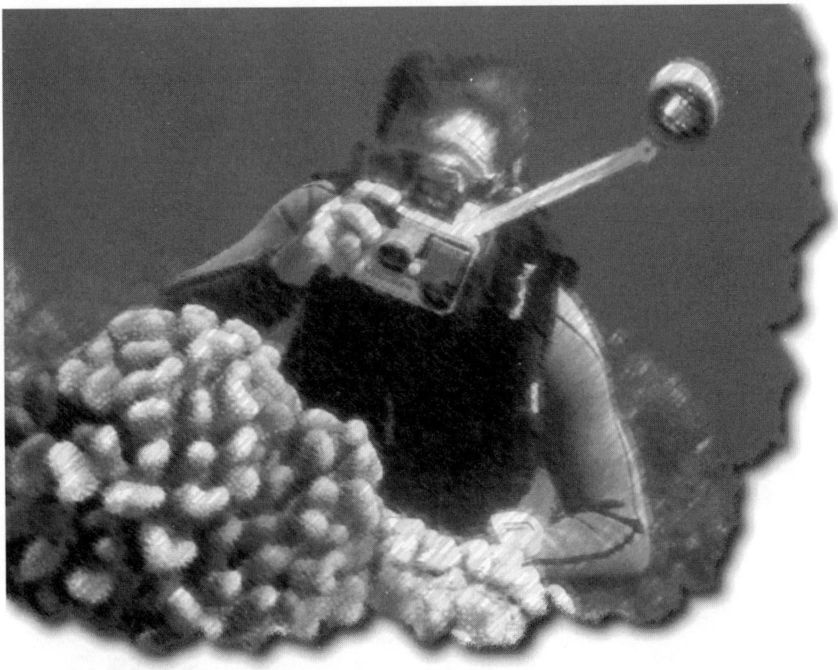

CHAPTER 1: GETTING STARTED

The desire to share our experiences with others is something most divers have in common. Underwater photography provides among the best and most enjoyable means for us to do so. Taking pictures under water can be a richly satisfying experience. It can also be an experience that is surprisingly easy to enjoy.

THE REWARDS OF UNDERWATER PHOTOGRAPHY

Here are several of the most common reasons divers take pictures under water:

- **Sharing With Others:** Photography makes it possible for us to share our experiences with divers and nondivers alike. It enables us to give fellow divers another perspective on the underwater world. It allows us to show nondiving friends and family members the unique opportunities they are missing. And it helps us tell stories (pictures are among the most powerful means of communication we have).

- **Enhancing Your Enjoyment of Diving:** In the process of discovering how to shoot pictures under water, we learn many new and valuable skills. These skills include improved buoyancy control and the ability to combine our basic diving abilities with other tasks (Figure 1-1). Perhaps most valuable, taking pictures teaches us to look at the underwater world in a whole new way. Many new underwater photographers report that their picture taking causes them to discover aquatic creatures and animal behaviors they somehow missed before.

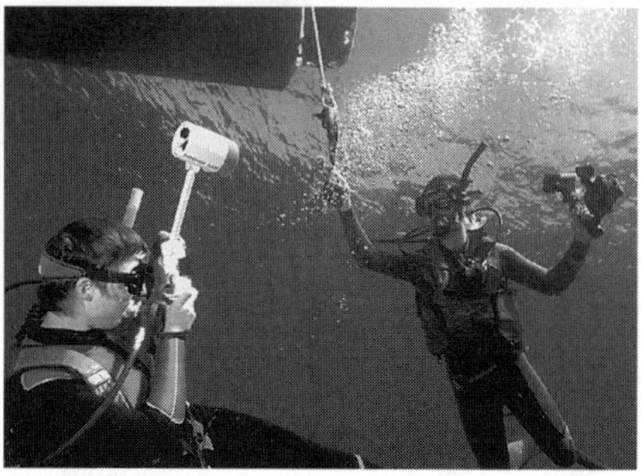

Figure 1-1 *Photography teaches you to combine excellent buoyancy control with other tasks.*

- **Saving Memories:** Each dive we make is unique. Each dive takes us into a realm few others share. Inevitably, though, each dive must end. When it does, our dives leave us with vivid, enjoyable memories.

  Over time, however, these memories fade. Taking pictures helps us preserve them. Pictures help us relive our most enjoyable underwater experiences again and again.

- **Creating Art:** Look at the walls in your home or workplace. Are these walls decorated with generic paintings, posters and photographs? Would these walls look better if they were decorated with vivid photographs of divers, fish and other aquatic life? Of course they would! Underwater photography gives us the ability to turn our everyday surroundings into galleries of underwater art.

- **Furthering Your Career:** If you dive professionally, either full- or part-time—or are considering doing so—your underwater photographic skills can help. Commercial divers find photography invaluable in documenting inspections and similar projects. Recreational diving educators regularly use underwater photography to promote classes and entertain customers. Underwater photography is also a highly enjoyable subject to teach. Diving Instructors seeking resort employment regularly discover that photography skills can greatly enhance their employability and income (Figure 1-2).

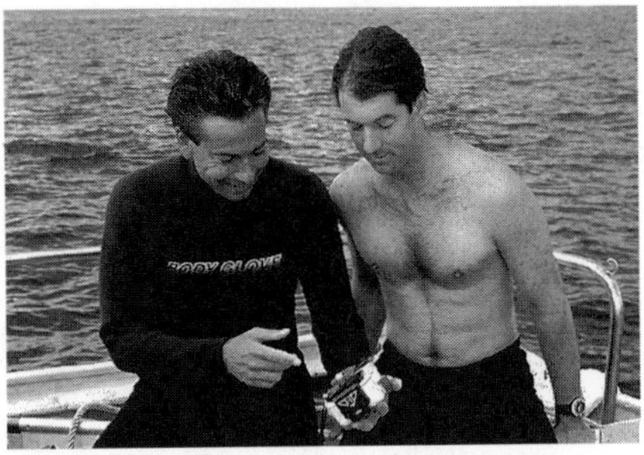

Figure 1-2 *Photo skills enhance opportunities for resort dive Instructors.*

If you are a writer and hope to sell diving related articles, being able to offer publishers underwater and topside photographs that match your text is essential. If you are a professional photographer or serious amateur, underwater photography can greatly expand your portfolio.

IT'S EASIER THAN YOU THINK

Given the benefits of underwater photography, it is surprising more divers do not carry cameras with them on every dive. Perhaps these divers mistakenly believe underwater photography is prohibitively expensive. Perhaps they think that basic underwater photographic skills are so complex as to be beyond their grasp. Possibly they are overwhelmed by the "techno-babble" with which experienced photographers sometimes intimidate beginners.

All these misconceptions are unfortunate, in that they discourage divers from discovering how enjoyable and rewarding underwater photography is. Here are the facts regarding how easy it is to get started in underwater imaging.

- **Underwater Photography Is Affordable:** While it is possible to spend a small fortune on underwater camera systems, it is also possible to start with only a modest investment. Underwater camera systems are modular. This means you can start with only the most basic components and build your system as your budget allows (Figure 1-3).

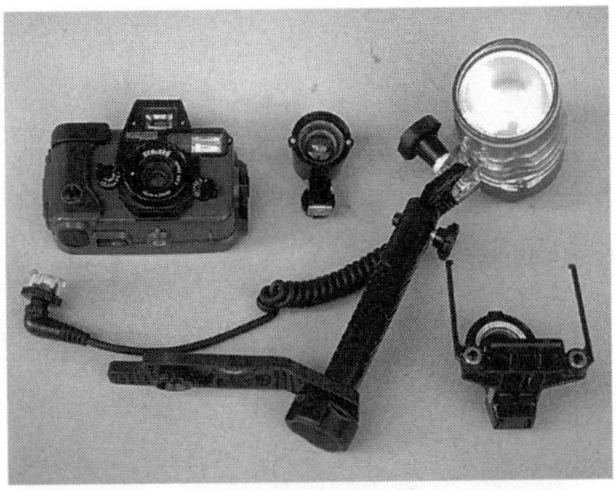

Figure 1-3 *The modularity of most camera systems enables you to start with the basics and build your camera system from there.*

Remember also that underwater photography greatly enhances the return you receive from the investment you made in first learning to dive.

- **Underwater Photography Can Be Easy:** You can take your first successful underwater photographs by following a few, easy steps. From there, underwater imaging can remain as simple or become as complex as you desire (Figure 1-4).

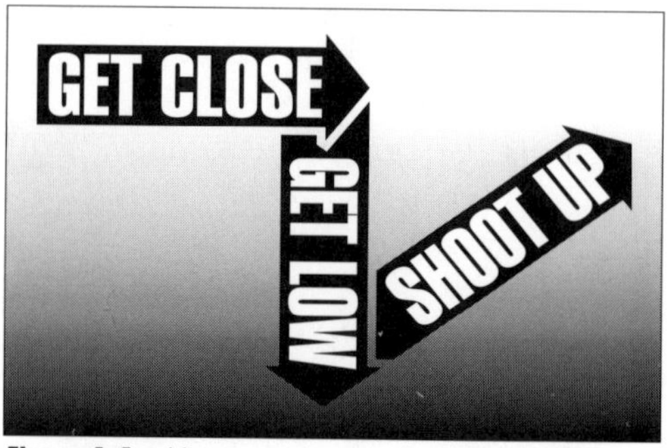

Figure 1-4 *You can take your first successful underwater photos by following a few, simple steps.*

- **Forget the Techno-Babble:** Understanding the basics of underwater photography requires mastering only a few, simple concepts. There are no complex formulas to remember and only a few, easily understood words to add to your vocabulary. If you want to go beyond this, you can; however, it is not necessary in order to get started.

We designed this book to help make your first underwater photo dives as easy and enjoyable as possible. Do not forget, however, that you should use the book in conjunction with the help and advice of your local SSI Dealer, and as part of a basic SSI *Underwater Photography* Specialty Course taught by that Dealer's staff of skilled SSI Instructors. Together, they can help you discover an entirely new and highly satisfying aspect of diving.

TASK LOADING: ITS IMPACT ON PHOTOGRAPHY AND ON SAFE, ENVIRONMENTALLY SOUND DIVING

Years ago, underwater photographers liked to point fingers at spearfishermen, wreck divers and others who allegedly had an adverse impact on the environment. Today, many dive resort operators will tell you that it is underwater photographers who seem to cause the greatest environmental damage.

Almost every dive resort operator you talk to has horror stories of underwater photographers who grab, stand on, sit on or crash into fragile

Your SSI Dealer: The Place to Start

You would not dream of trying to learn to drive, fly or dive simply by reading a book. Yet, every year, countless divers invest hundreds or thousands of dollars in underwater photographic equipment—only to gamble that investment on their ability to teach themselves to shoot pictures by reading a book or by trial and error. That is just plain silly.

Before spending a dime on underwater camera equipment that may not be what you really need, you should take advantage of the help and advice your local SSI Dealer can offer you. Doing so can save you hundreds or even thousands of dollars.

Odds are, your local SSI Dealer has one or more staff members whose knowledge and experience in underwater photography far eclipses that of anyone you can talk to at your local camera store or at a mail-order camera distributor (Figure 1-A). These staff members can help you learn faster—and help you avoid costly, time-consuming mistakes.

You should also get as much formal training as you can before spending money on equipment. Many SSI Dealers offer ongoing photo seminars and regularly scheduled Underwater Photography Specialty Diver courses. If you think back to when you first learned to dive, you probably remember being much more confident about buying your basic dive gear after having the opportunity to try a variety of equipment items in the pool. You will find that the same is true of underwater photo equipment.

Learning to shoot great underwater photos is easy and fun—but it is not something you can learn simply by reading. Like learning to dive, it takes the one-on-one guidance, practice and supervision that only your local SSI dive center can provide.

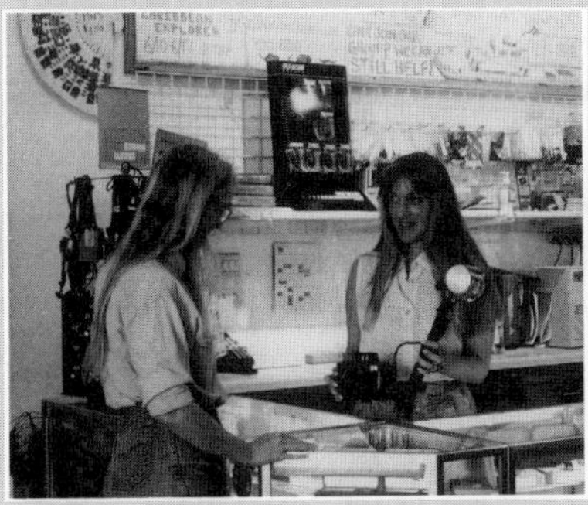

Figure 1-A *Odds are, your local SSI retailer has one or more staff members with expertise in underwater photography.*

corals while attempting to take pictures. They can show you where each of their dive sites has been defaced by careless, over-eager and seemingly unconcerned photographers. Obviously, divers who have so little control over their buoyancy and body movement also lack the control necessary to take good pictures. Additionally, if they are so focused on their cameras that they ignore what is going on around them, it is also unlikely they are paying sufficient attention to such important factors as air supply, depth, time, direction and where their buddies are.

Underwater photography places a considerable task load on the unprepared. While taking good pictures can be a matter of following a few, simple steps, you must first achieve total mastery of such basic diving skills as buoyancy control, body position and propulsion. These skills must become automatic, requiring little or no conscious thought. Only then can you concentrate on the steps needed to take good pictures while continuing to be a safe, environmentally sound diver.

In Chapter 4, we discuss how to assess your present diving skills to see if you possess the level of control necessary to enter the water with a camera and not be a danger to yourself and the environment. We also outline several exercises you can practice in your dive center's pool or at you local dive site to better prepare you for the first time you enter the water with a camera.

HOW FILM AND CAMERAS WORK

Your ability to take successful underwater photographs starts with a basic understanding of how film and cameras work. You do not need a university degree in the technology of imaging; however, there are a few simple concepts that will help you better understand why it is important to do certain things when taking underwater photographs.

How Film Works

Modern photographic film is nothing more than a long strip of celluloid with a special coating. The basic component of this coating is silver hydride. Its chief property is that it reacts in a variety of ways when exposed to differing quantities of light.

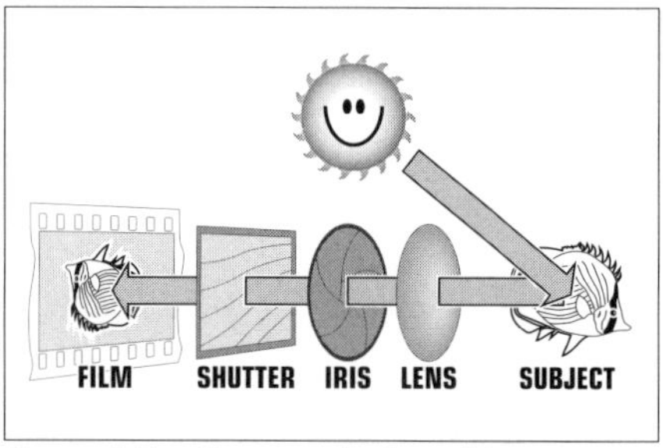

Figure 1-5 *Photography is nothing more than exposing frames of film to the right quantity of sharply focused light.*

When we take photos, we do nothing more than make certain that we expose the film to the right quantity of light, so that its chemical coating reacts the way we want. Additionally, we must make certain that the light we expose the film to is precisely focused, so that the resulting images are sharp and easy to recognize (Figure 1-5).

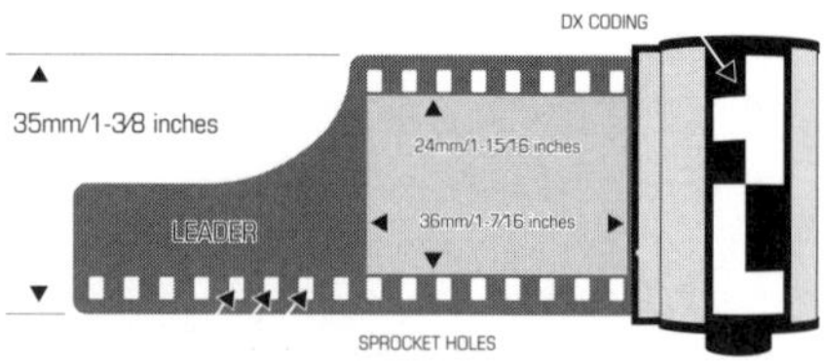

Figure 1-6 *35mm is by far the most popular format for film.*

Photographic film has three other properties with which you should be familiar.

- **Size:** The *35mm* film format is by far the most popular for both surface and underwater photography. Professional underwater photographers occasionally use the large-format film common to studio photography. Nevertheless, the vast majority of underwater photos you see published in books and magazines are taken using 35mm film (Figure 1-6).

- **Type:** Thirty-five millimetre film falls into two broad categories. *Print film,* when developed, becomes negatives from which photo labs can make prints in a variety of sizes. *Reversal (slide) film,* when developed, turns directly into color transparencies. Photographers usually have their photo lab mount these transparencies in slide frames, so that they may view them using a slide projector or other devices. Photo labs can also use transparencies to make high quality color prints.

  Print film is available in either color or black and white. Color print film often has the word *color* in its name, such as Koda*color* or Fuji*color.*

  Reversal film is only available in color. Reversal films often have the word *chrome* in their name, such as Koda*chrome*, Ekta*chrome* and Fuji*chrome.*

- **Speed:** Photographers rate film according to its sensitivity to light. So-called "slow" films require more light for adequate exposures, but yield brighter, richer colors (photographers call this better *color saturation*) and finer detail (called finer *grain*). Conversely, "fast" films require less light for adequate exposures, but do so with less color saturation. Additionally, when you examine these films closely, you detect a noticeably coarser grain, yielding less detail (Figure 1-7).

  Film manufacturers rate the speed of film using ISO (International Standards Organization) numbers (Figure 1-8). This system replaces the old ASA rating

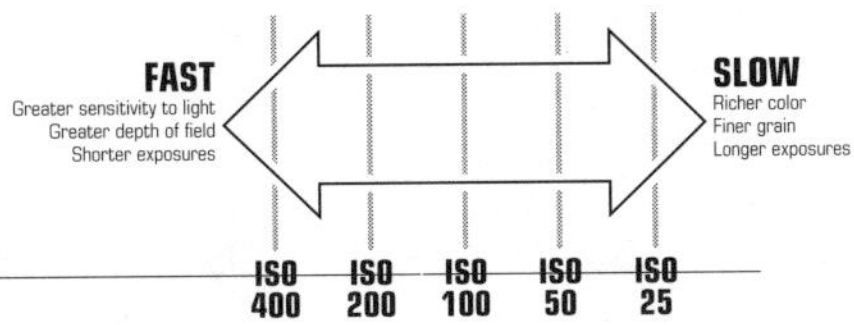

Figure 1-7 *"Slow" films are less sensitive to light, but offer better color saturation and finer grain. (Note: Each increment in ISO shown here represents a doubling or halving in a film's sensitivity to light).*

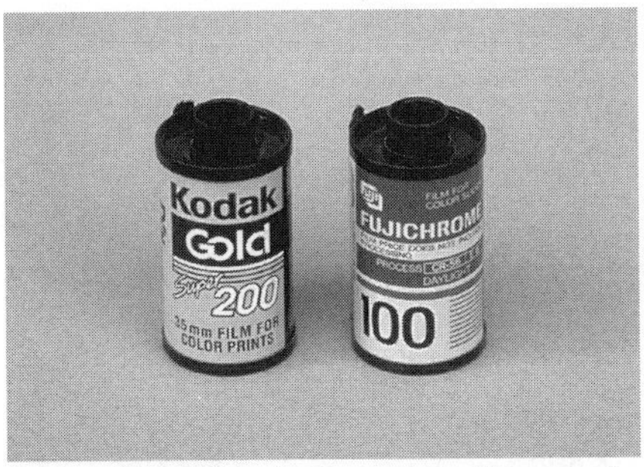

Figure 1-8 *Manufacturers rate film speed using the ISO rating system.*

system that was common in North America a few years ago. Slower films have lower ISO numbers; faster films have higher ISO numbers. Underwater photographers most often use ISO 100 film. For special applications, however, they may use film as slow as ISO 64, 50 or 25, or as fast as ISO 400.

At the end of Chapter 2, we cover the advantages and drawbacks of various types of film, and discuss how to choose the best film for your needs.

How Cameras Work

Your underwater camera is essentially a light-proof box with a hole in it, through which controlled quantities of light can pass. Its function is to help you expose the film inside to just the right quantity of precisely focused light. All cameras, no matter how simple or complex, have four basic components (Figure 1-9). These are:

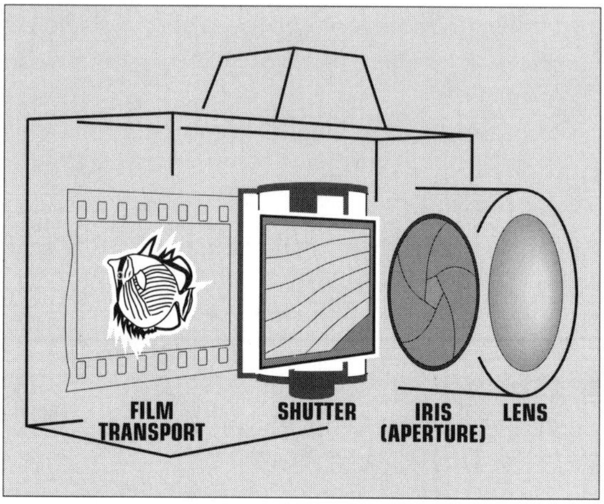

Figure 1-9 *All cameras, no matter how simple or complex, have these four basic components.*

- **Lens:** Your camera's lens focuses light rays on the film. Camera lenses range widely in complexity and function.

  The simplest cameras have non-focusable lenses. These are pre-set to the range of distances at which the average consumer most commonly takes pictures above water. Typically, subject matter must be from six to ten feet (two to three metres), in bright light, to be in focus.

  Most underwater photographers use cameras that have focusable lenses. They can focus these lenses to cover a wide range of distances. You can set the focus on the lenses found on most underwater cameras to distances ranging from less than three feet (one metre) to infinity.

  These days, most housed *Single-Lens Reflex* (SLR) camera systems (described later in Chapter 2) use *autofocus* lenses. These focus on subject matter automatically and work well under water. They are particularly well suited for aquatic animal portraits (Figure 1-10).

The vast majority of underwater camera systems use *fixed-focal-length* lenses. The term *fixed focal length* refers to the fact these lenses' *angle of acceptance* ("angle of coverage" or, the area the lens sees) is not adjustable. This is the opposite of a zoom lens. With a fixed-focal-length lens, the guide to its angle of coverage is its *focal-length measurement*. The cameras most divers use come with 35mm lenses. It is easy to assume this number has something to do with the 35mm film the camera uses. It does not. Instead, it generally refers to the distance from optical center of the rear-most lens element to the film.

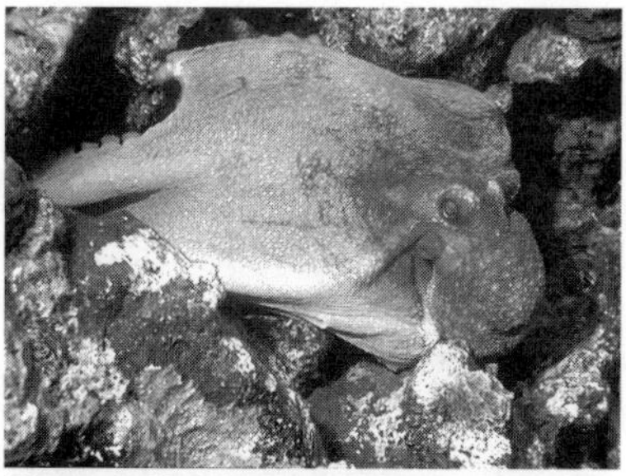

Figure 1-10 *Housed SLR cameras are particularly well-suited for aquatic animal portraits.*

A 35mm underwater lens typically has an angle of acceptance equal to roughly two-thirds of what the human eye can see. In this respect, it is comparable to the 50mm lenses that come with many topside cameras. This frustrates many divers when their eyes see an underwater scene they would like to shoot, but they discover their lens is only capable of capturing a portion of it (Figure 1-11).

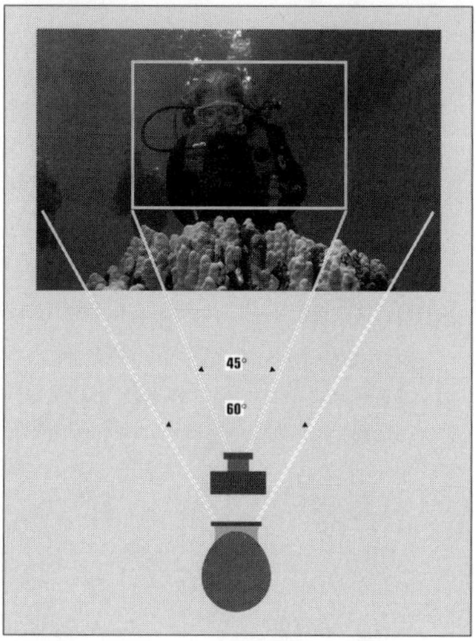

Figure 1-11 *The typical underwater camera lens only sees a portion of what the human eye can at the same distance.*

An additional limiting factor of 35mm underwater lenses is that they have a relatively narrow *depth-of-field*. This refers to the range of distances in which subject matter will be in focus (Figure 1-12).

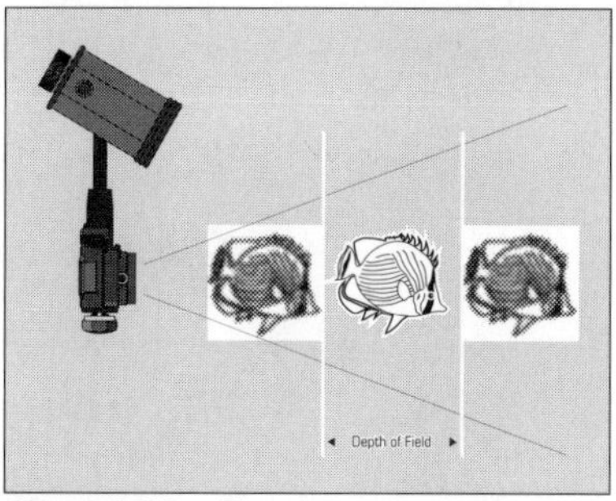

Figure 1-12 *The term "depth of field" refers to the zone in which subjects will be in sharpest focus.*

A solution to these problems is to use an accessory lens with a wider angle of coverage. A 28mm lens has an angle of acceptance roughly equivalent to the human eye. Even wider lenses are available. Fifteen millimetre lenses are a favorite of professional photographers. They capture more light, make murky water appear clear and have a depth of field that is nearly infinite. We discuss wide-angle photography in more depth in Chapter 5.

- **Aperture:** Behind your camera's lens is an opening whose diameter determines how much light can pass into the camera body and on to the film. This is the *aperture* (Figure 1-13). The simplest cameras have *fixed apertures.* As with these cameras' fixed-focus lenses, the intention here is to create an inexpensive way to capture images in the range most consumers shoot above water, without any need for adjustments.

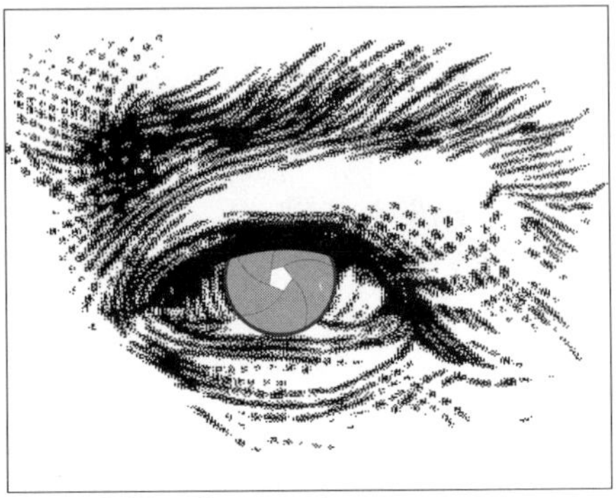

Figure 1-13 *A camera's aperture mechanism is much like the iris of the human eye.*

Most underwater camera systems have an adjustable aperture or *iris.* This enables divers to control the quantity of light reaching the film at any shutter speed. We measure aperture in units called *f*-stops. Lower *f*-stops represent wider apertures, and let more light reach the film. Conversely, higher *f*-stops represent smaller apertures and let less light reach the film. As you move up the *f*-stop scale, each increasing stop represents a reduction in aperture size that allows half as much light to reach the film as the previous stop. For example, an aperture setting of *f*8 results in only half as much light reaching the film as at the next lower aperture setting, *f*5.6 (Figure 1-14).

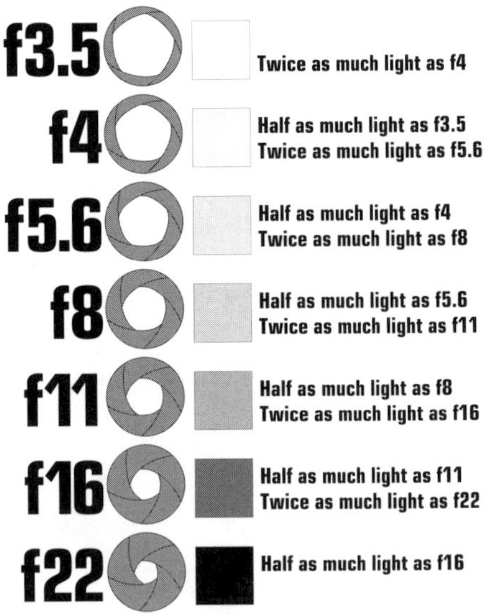

Figure 1-14 *F-stop relationships.*

- **Shutter:** The very first silver-coated photographic plates of the nineteenth century required exposure times of up to ten minutes or more. In contrast, today's films require exposure times measured in tenths, hundredths or even thousandths of a second. With such sensitivity, modern cameras obviously require highly precise mechanisms to control how long they expose each frame of film to light.

  The mechanism which enables this is the *shutter*. The moving parts of the shutter are called *shutter leaves* (Figure 1-15). The movement of the shutter leaves ensures that the camera exposes each portion of the frame to light for exactly the same duration.

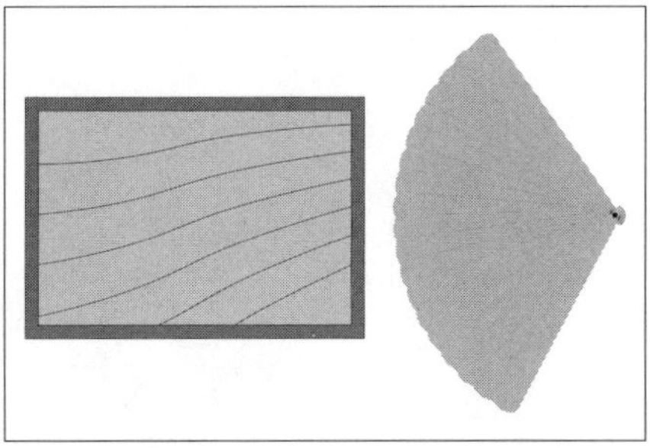

Figure 1-15 *The shutter mechanism found in most cameras operates much like the blades of a folding fan.*

  We measure the amount of time the shutter exposes each frame to light in fractions of a second. *Shutter speeds* can range from as slow as one second or longer, to as fast a 1/1,000th of a second or faster. Typical shutter speeds used underwater range from 1/30th to 1/125th of a second (Figure 1-16).

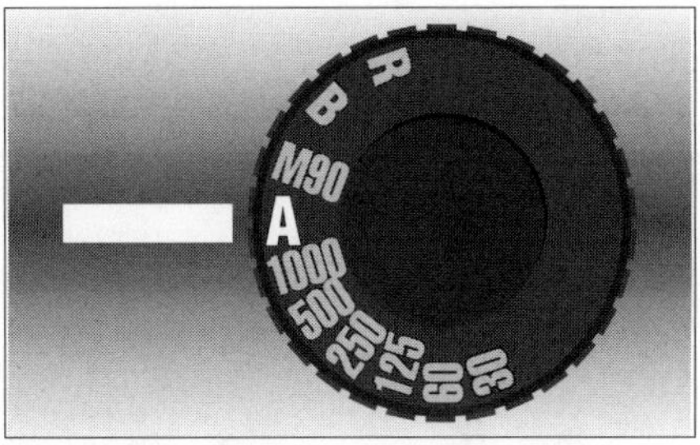

Figure 1-16 *Many underwater camera systems offer a wide range of shutter speeds.*

  As you may know, or have realized by now, both shutter speed and aperture are capable of controlling the quantity of light reaching the film. For a more detailed discussion of how shutter speed and aperture relate to one another, and how this relationship impacts our exposure decisions, see the accompanying article, *The Exposure See-Saw*, page 12.

- **Film Transport:** To expose each frame on a roll of film to light, a camera must have a means of moving each frame to the proper position on the camera's *focal plane*. This is the two-dimensional area behind the lens, aperture and shutter on which the light entering the camera body will be in proper focus. This mechanism must be reasonably precise, so that exposed frames do not overlap one another and are evenly spaced along the entire roll of film. Additionally, this mechanism must help prevent accidental exposure to light.

The Exposure See-Saw

By now you know from your reading that both aperture and shutter speed can control the amount of light that reaches your film. It is logical, therefore, to ask how these two factors relate to one another.

As the text describes, changing your aperture by one *f*-stop either doubles or halves the amount of light that reaches your film. Doubling or halving your shutter speed accomplishes the same thing. What this means is that for any given *exposure value* (the overall amount of light needed for a proper exposure), there will be several combinations of shutter speed and aperture that will achieve the goal of exposing the film to the right amount of light.

The chart in Figure 1-B is an example of this principle at work. In clear, shallow ocean water, a common exposure value is *f*5.6 for 1/60th of a second. As the chart shows, you achieve the same exposure by shooting at *f*8 for 1/30th of a second, or *f*4 for 1/125th of a second. There is literally a see-saw effect: as *f*-stop increases, shutter speed must decrease; as shutter speed increases, *f*-stops must decrease.

Given this flexibility, how do you choose which factor to increase and which to decrease? When you increase shutter speed, you gain the ability to freeze action. This is why sports photographers like to shoot at the fastest speeds possible. Fast shutter speeds are also helpful in situations where it is difficult to hold the camera still. In both instances, faster shutter speeds work to help reduce the possibility of blurred photos.

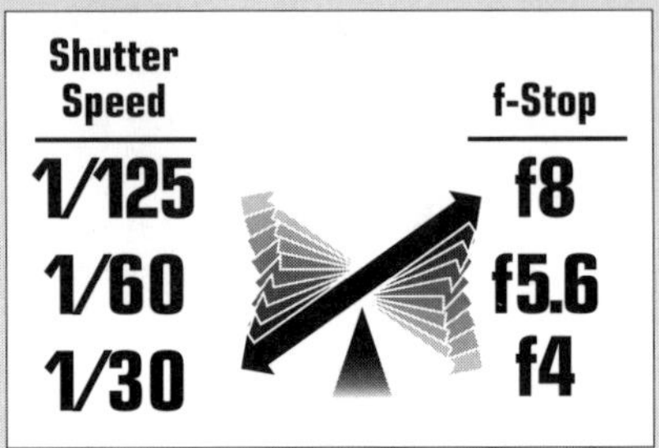

Figure 1-B *The Exposure See-Saw.*

The chief benefit of using higher *f*-stops is that, in doing so, you gain depth of field. This is the range in which your subject matter will be in sharpest focus. As Figure 1-C shows, with a 35mm lens set for three feet (one metre), by closing your aperture just one *f*-stop, you increase your depth of field by nearly 100%.

As underwater photographers, it is

The photographic community calls the camera mechanism that enables this to take place the *film transport*. There two basic types of film transport mechanisms: *manual* and *motor-driven*. Many divers prefer one type of mechanism over the other.

For example, some divers like the convenience of a motor drive due to the fact it requires fewer potentially-fish-distracting hand movements. Others prefer the simplicity and reliability of a manual advance. Both mechanisms are suitable for underwater photography. Both employ such components as *sprockets, take-up spools* and *rewind* mechanisms, with which you must become familiar to properly load and unload film.

more important for us to increase depth of field than it is for us to freeze action. Seldom, if ever, do we shoot fast moving action under water. Additionally, with the exception of shooting in surgy conditions (something you should avoid as a beginner), it is generally easier to hold a camera still under water than it is on the surface.

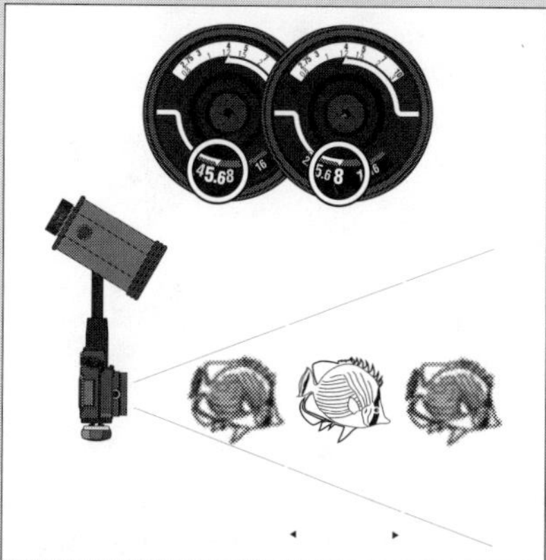

Figure 1-C *Closing your aperture just one f-stop can nearly double your depth of field.*

On the other hand, there is usually so little light underwater that we have to shoot at much lower *f*-stops than we do on the surface. This makes gaining whatever depth of field we can a priority.

If there were no underwater strobes or other artificial light sources, we would be limited to shooting with available light. In this case, we would want to shoot at as slow a shutter speed as possible, so that we could use the highest possible *f*-stop. Fortunately, we have strobes, and they enable us to use higher *f*-stops than ambient light generally allows.

As a beginning underwater photographer, you will most likely shoot using your camera system's *TTL* (Through The Lens) exposure metering system. We describe this in greater detail on page 17. One aspect of TTL strobe photography is that, on most cameras, it locks your shutter speed at 1⁄60th, 1⁄90th, 1⁄100th or 1⁄125th of a second.

As you no longer have control over shutter speed, the distance to your primary subject will now dictate your *f*-stop. The closer you can get, the more the strobe light can reach the subject, enabling you to use a higher *f*-stop to gain more depth of field.

This is yet another reason why the first of the three basic principles of underwater photography we cover in Chapter 4 is *Get Close.*

Additionally, most underwater camera systems have three additional features of which you should be aware. They are:

- **Viewfinder:** The *viewfinder* is what we look through to help make sure our subject matter is properly centered and will fill the frame the way we want. Their are three basic types of viewfinders: *rangefinder, external* and *Single-Lens Reflex* (SLR).

  Rangefinders are common on the amphibious cameras we discuss in Chapter 2. A rangefinder is a small opening on the back of the camera body with a corresponding opening in the front. Looking through the rangefinder gives you an approximate idea of what the lens sees (Figure 1-17, page 14).

The chief benefit of rangefinders is their simplicity and low cost. The chief drawbacks of rangefinders are their small size and the fact they suffer from something called *parallax error,* which we will discuss shortly.

Some divers have difficulty seeing through rangefinders. The distance between these divers' eyes and the lens of their masks increases this problem.

Parallax error results from the fact rangefinders are never perfectly in line with the center of the camera's lens. As a result, what you see through the rangefinder is not precisely what the lens sees. This can result in off-center photographs (Figure 1-18). To help you avoid this problem, most rangefinders have *parallax correction marks* to help you compensate (Figure 1-19).

External viewfinders mount to the top of the camera or housing. They range from simple framers to high-quality optical viewfinders with multiple lens elements (Figure 1-20). The chief benefit of external viewfinders is that they are generally much larger and, thus, easier to look through than internal rangefinders. They are also generally the only means divers have to properly frame subject matter when shooting amphibious cameras with wide-angle lenses.

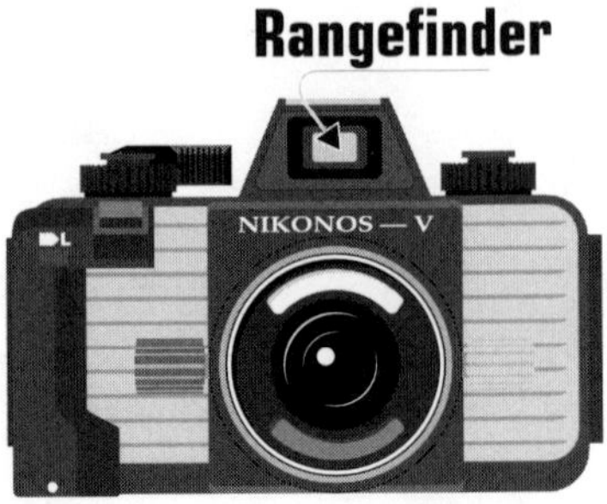

Figure 1-17 *Most amphibious cameras have a rangefinder located at the top of the camera body.*

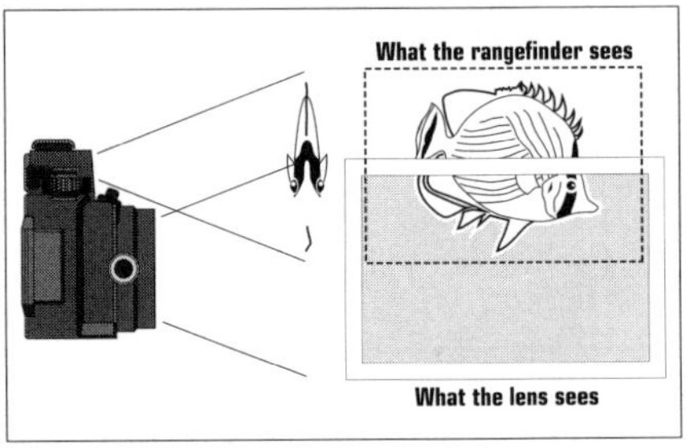

Figure 1-18 *Parallax error results from the rangefinder being off-center from the lens.*

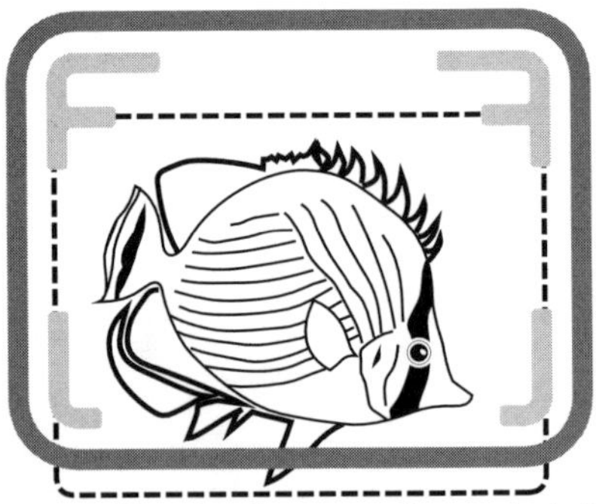

Figure 1-19 *Parallax correction marks help you align close-up subjects with the center of the lens.*

The chief drawback of external viewfinders is that, because they mount to the outside of the camera or housing, they greatly increase the problem of parallax error. To compensate for the increased parallax, external viewfinders may employ parallax marks, as do rangefinders, or they may feature a *parallax adjustment dial*. The adjustment dial enables you to tilt the viewfinder so that it aims at the same point on your subject matter that the camera lens does.

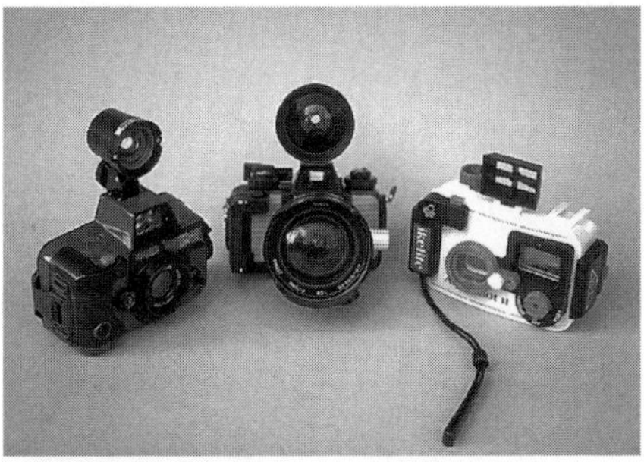

Figure 1-20 *Cameras equipped with external viewfinders.*

The third type of view finder is that found in *Single-Lens-Reflex* (SLR) cameras. This type of viewfinder allows you to actually look through the camera's lens to compose your shot. Obviously, this type of system eliminates parallax error. To use it, however, you must have an SLR camera in a housing.

As with all camera systems, these have both advantages and drawbacks. You will learn more about SLR and other underwater camera systems in Chapter 2.

- **Strobe:** As we discuss in Chapter 2, among the many challenges of shooting film under water is how little natural light is available there. This lack of light makes an artificial light source essential to provide adequate lighting and to restore natural looking color.

  In the early days of underwater photography, divers used flash bulbs to provide this light source. You can imagine how impractical this was—not to mention the impact of loose flash bulbs on the environment.

  Today, divers use electronic flashes or *strobes*. These are much more convenient to use and environmentally safe. Strobes consist of four basic components: a *sync cord* or *slave sensor; a power supply;* one or more *capacitors;* and one or more *flash tubes* (Figure 1-21).

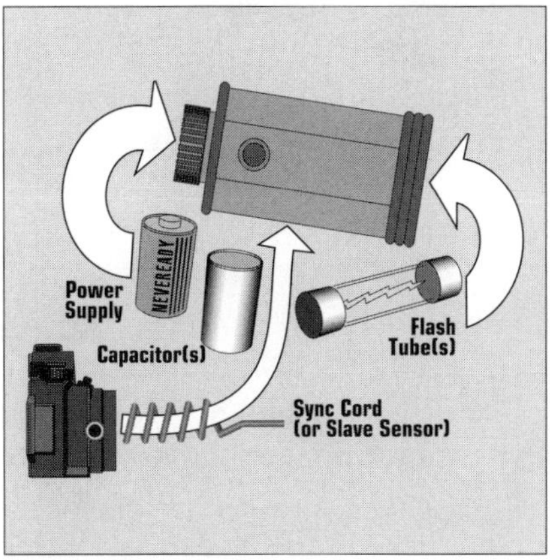

Figure 1-21 *The four basic components of underwater strobes.*

  Strobes release an incredibly bright burst of light whose total duration lasts less than 1/100th of a second (some strobes flashes may last only

1/10,000th of a second). To be effective, the entire duration of this burst must occur during that fraction of a second when the camera's shutter is completely open. We call this being in *sync* (short for synchronization). To achieve this, strobes use one of two activating mechanisms.

The most common of these mechanisms is a *sync cord* (Figure 1-22). The first electronic signal the sync cord sends to the strobe tells it to begin firing. Many sync cords also send a second signal that tells the strobe when to stop firing.

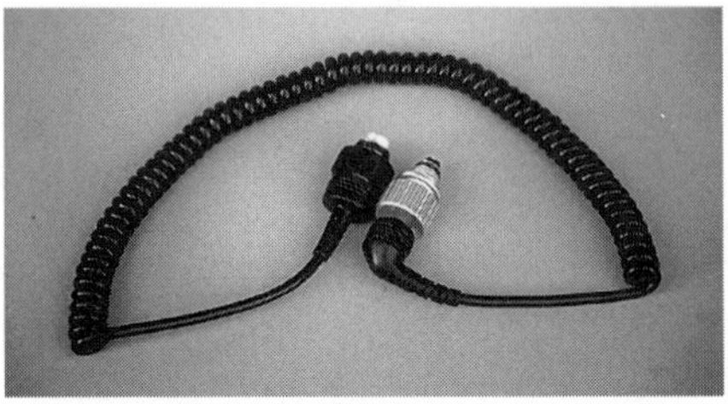

Figure 1-22 *Sync cord.*

Some strobes use an activation device called a *slave sensor.* This sensor triggers the strobe when it detects a burst of light from another source (Figure 1-23). A common application of this technology is to have a model hold a strobe, equipped with a slave sensor, as though it was a dive light. When the photographer's main strobe fires, the slave strobe will fire simultaneously. The resulting picture will create the illusion that the model was holding an underwater light.

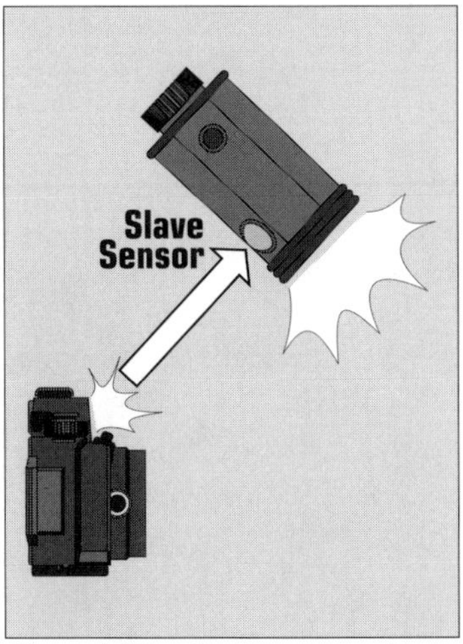

Figure 1-23 *Slave sensors trigger a strobe when they detect the flash of another strobe.*

All strobes require an energy source. This can be either alkaline or rechargeable batteries. There are some strobes that only work with the rechargeable ni-cad battery packs that come with them. Other strobes can use either standard alkaline batteries or their consumer-rechargeable equivalents (Figure 1-24).

No reasonably-sized battery pack—no matter how powerful—can provide enough energy, over a fraction of a second, for the strobe to output sufficient light. For this reason, strobes use devices called *capacitors.* Capacitors can store all the energy a strobe's battery pack normally outputs in six to ten seconds, then release that energy in one blinding, fraction-of-a-second-long burst.

The strobe's capacitors direct their energy output to special electrical bulbs called *flash tubes*. Flash tubes are capable of emitting blinding bursts of light of very short duration. In smaller strobes, flash tubes are typically short and cylindrical. Larger strobes may use circular flash tubes or multiple shorter tubes.

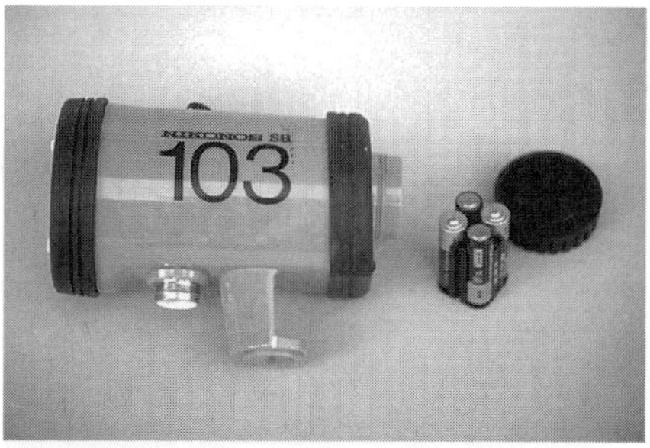

Figure 1-24 *Strobes may use alkaline or rechargeable batteries.*

Strobes may also have a built-in or accessory cover for the flash tube called a *diffuser* (Figure 1-25). Diffusers can widen the flash tube's area of coverage—useful for wide-angle shots. They can also soften some flash tubes' tendency to create *hot spots* (uneven light distribution). Diffusers are not without their drawbacks. They can reduce a strobe's total light output by 50 percent. Some experienced photographers like to use diffusers. Some do not.

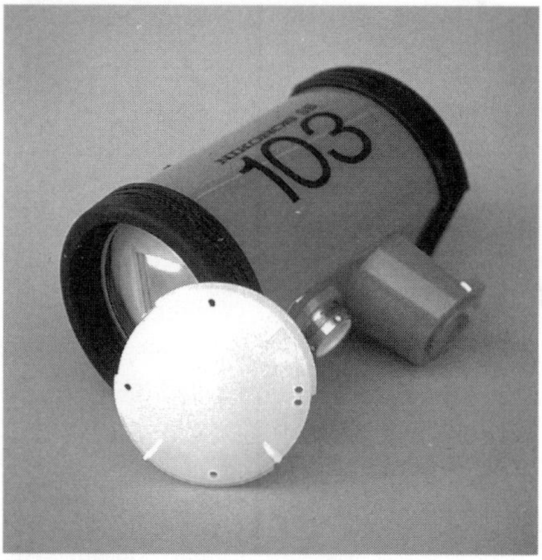

Figure 1-25 *Strobe diffuser.*

A final strobe accessory is an *aiming light,* which helps photographers point the strobe in the right direction. We cover these in greater detail in Chapter 4.

- **Metering System:** All but the simplest of today's underwater camera systems have built-in *metering* systems to help control exposures. In fact, most cameras have two metering systems.

  One metering system typically dedicates itself solely to available light photos. It usually measures the amount of light entering the lens, then adjusts the shutter speed for a proper exposure.

  The vast majority of underwater photos require use of a strobe. Thus, what most underwater photographers rely on is the *TTL* (Through The Lens) strobe metering system. This system couples, through a special sync cord, to the strobe's TTL circuitry.

Here is how the system works: When the shutter opens, the camera signals the strobe to begin firing. Light from the strobe bounces off the subject and returns to the camera. When the TTL circuitry inside the camera senses that sufficient light has reached the film (a condition known as *quenching),* it sends a signal to the strobe to cease firing. All this happens well within the tiny fraction of a second the strobe normally takes to release its full output (Figure 1-26).

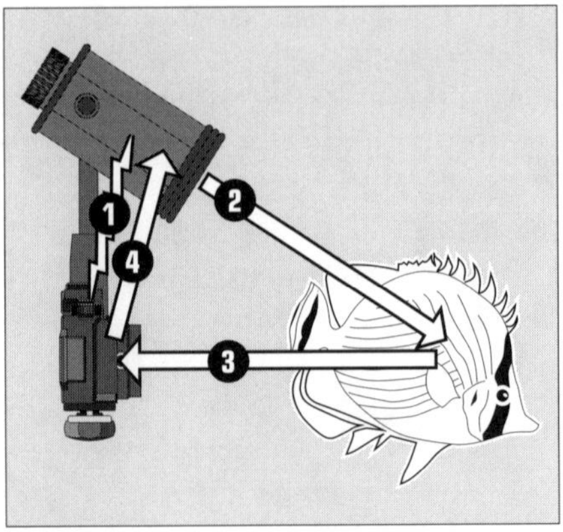

Figure 1-26 *1&2—Depressing the shutter sends a signal to the TTL strobe to begin firing; 3—when sufficient light bounces off the subject, 4—the SPD sensor inside the camera tells the strobe to stop firing.*

Although TTL technology advances rapidly, no metering system is perfect. This is particularly true of the amphibious cameras most underwater photographers use—and especially when these cameras are used with wide-angle lenses. For this reason, many experienced underwater photographers prefer to control their exposures manually.

Nevertheless, using your camera's TTL circuitry will result in acceptable exposures most of the time. For this reason, most Instructors recommend that you stick with TTL photography when first starting out. It reduces your overall task load, and enables you to concentrate on distance to subject, composition, strobe angle and—most important of all—safe, environmentally sound diving.

CHAPTER 1 REVIEW

1. While taking good pictures can be a matter of following a few, simple steps, you must first achieve total mastery of such basic diving skills as ______________________, ______________ ______________________, and ________________.

2. Your ability to take successful underwater photographs starts with a basic understanding of how ______________________________________.

3. When we take photos, we do nothing more than make certain that we expose the film to the ______________________________________, so that its chemical coating reacts the way we want.

4. Most underwater photographers use cameras that have focusable lenses. They can focus these lenses to cover a ___________________________ ______________________________________.

5. Behind your camera's lens is an opening whose diameter determines how much light can pass into the camera body and onto the film. This is ________________________.

6. ______________________ represent wider apertures, and let more light reach the film. Conversely, ______________________ represent smaller apertures and let less light reach the film.

7. Parallax error results from the fact that rangefinders are never perfectly in line with the ______ ______________________.

8. All but the simplest of today's underwater camera systems have built-in metering systems to ______ ______________________.

9. The first electronic signal the sync cord sends to the strobe tells it to ______________________ ______________________.

10. When the TTL circuitry inside the camera senses that sufficient light has reached the film, it sends a signal to the strobe to ______________________ ______________________.

Selecting the Right Equipment & Film

2

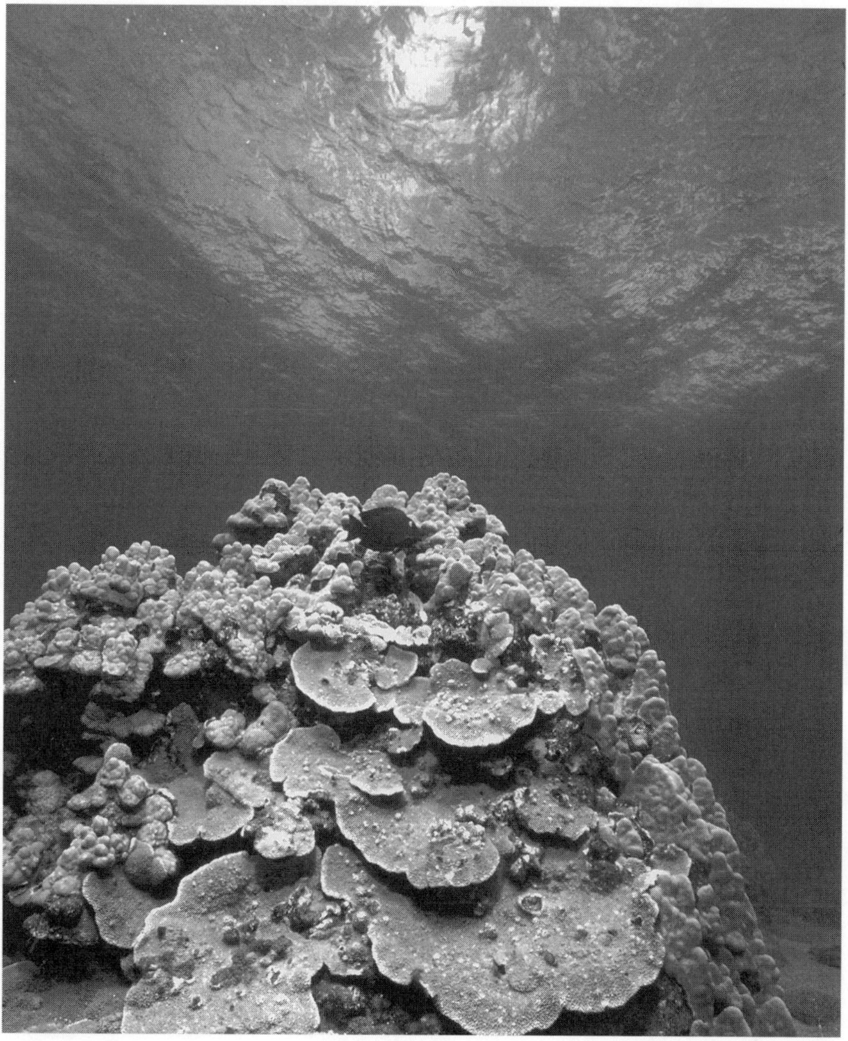

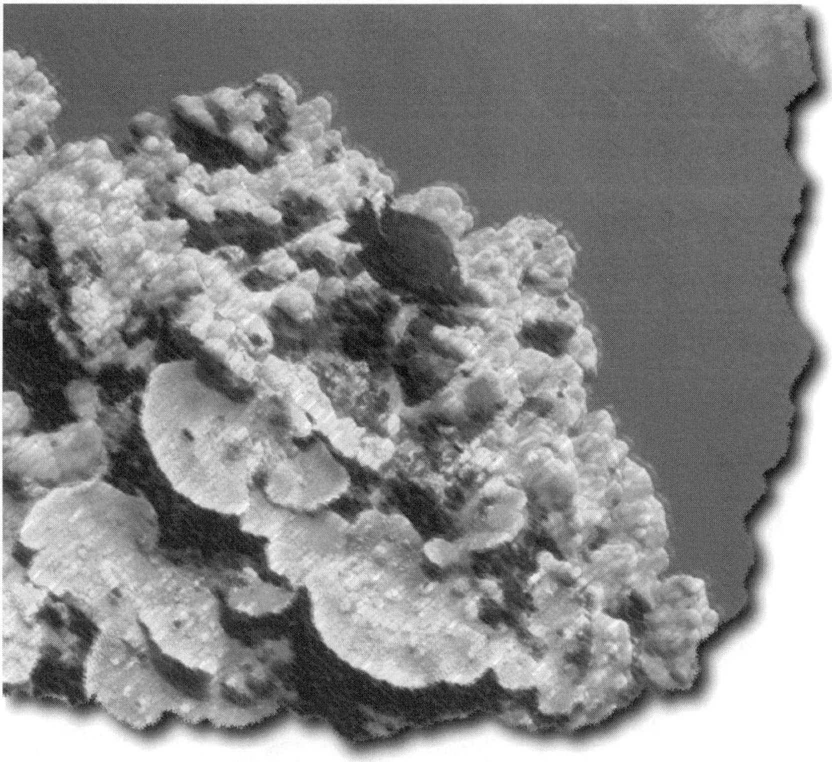

CHAPTER 2: SELECTING THE RIGHT EQUIPMENT AND FILM

As a beginner, you will find shooting good pictures under water can be surprisingly easy—if you follow a few, basic steps. It is not, however, as automatic a process as many of today's point-and-shoot cameras make topside photography. If you want to take good underwater pictures, you must first understand the challenges you will face and the equipment you will need. You will then be better equipped to succeed.

DETERMINING WHAT IS BEST FOR YOU

"What is the best underwater camera system?" This is much like asking, "What is the best car?" or, "What is the most delicious food?" There is no single underwater camera system that is the best for everybody. There is only the camera system that is best for you.

Porsches and Ferraris are unquestionably excellent automobiles; however, this fact does you little good if what you really need is a station wagon or van (Figure 2-1). The same basic principle applies to underwater cameras.

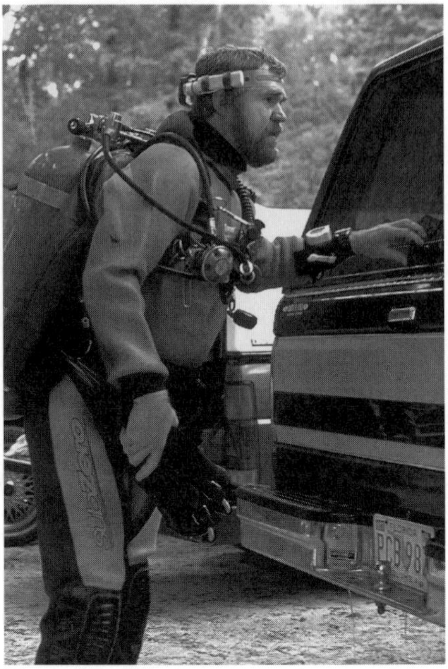

Figure 2-1 *The most expensive sports car made is of little value if your type of diving requires a pick-up truck. The same principle applies to camera selection; a system is only "best" if it meets your specific needs.*

As we mentioned earlier in Chapter 1, you can no more learn to take underwater pictures solely by reading a book than you can learn to dive, fly or drive by reading a book. You are going to have to rely on the knowledge and experience of the folks at your local SSI Dealer to help you get the most from whatever camera system you buy. Obviously, it makes sense to purchase a system with which your local SSI Dealer is familiar, and with which they have considerable experience.

Equally important, you should purchase a camera system based on its ability to take the kind of pictures you want. Not every underwater camera system can take every kind of underwater picture. Some systems may require the purchase of special lenses or accessories before they can take the kind of pictures you want (Figure 2-2). Other systems may simply never be capable of taking the particular type of pictures that interest you.

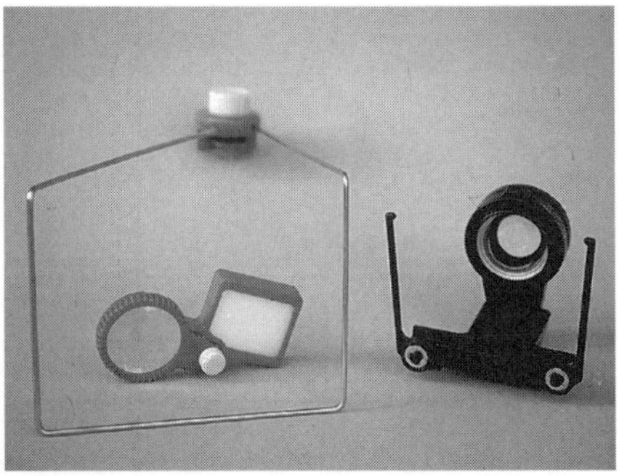

Figure 2-2 *Some camera systems require the purchase of special lenses or accessories to enable you to take the kind of pictures you want.*

Common sense dictates that the more expensive a camera system is, the more capabilities it will have. This does not mean you necessarily have to spend a fortune getting into underwater photography. If the system you select has sufficient potential for growth, you can start small and expand your system's capabilities as your budget allows.

What Type of Pictures Do You Want To Take?

The first step in purchasing the right underwater camera system for you is to make a realistic assessment of the type of pictures you want to take. Armed with this information, you can then determine which of the available camera systems can take these pictures.

Here is an overview of five different picture categories. Following this, you will read about the three basic types of underwater camera systems. Finally, you will find a chart that shows you which types of shots each different camera system is capable of taking.

- **Diver Portrait and Marine Still Life Shots:** Later in this chapter, we discuss the challenges of shooting film under water. In that discussion we point out that, for best results, your primary subject must be within three to four feet (one to one-and-a-quarter metres) of the camera. At this distance, the standard 35mm lens found on many underwater camera systems covers an area no larger than roughly two feet by three feet (60cm by 90cm) (Figure 2-3). To get an idea of how big this is, imagine a medium-size picture frame, floating in space just outside arm's reach.

  At first, this may seem fairly limiting. It does, after all, cover only a small percentage of what your eyes can see at this distance.

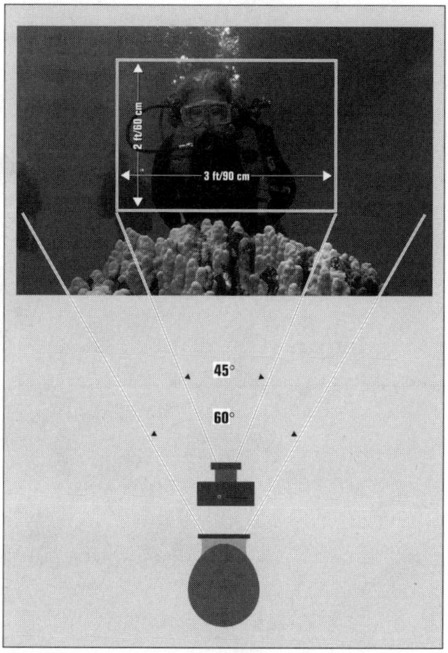

Figure 2-3 *What our eyes see is not necessarily what the camera sees. At our normal shooting distance (arm's length from the camera) most standard underwater lenses can only capture an area the size of a medium picture frame; this is a fraction of what we can see with our eyes at the same distance.*

Nevertheless, there is quite a bit of fascinating subject matter that can fit within this space.

You can, for example, take head-and-shoulders portraits of your dive buddy looking at the camera, holding small objects such as artifacts or shells, or closely examining coral formations. You can also do still-life shots of medium-size objects such as sea fans, basket sponges or coral heads. Yet another shot that fits within these size constraints is one depicting a school of fish (Figure 2-4).

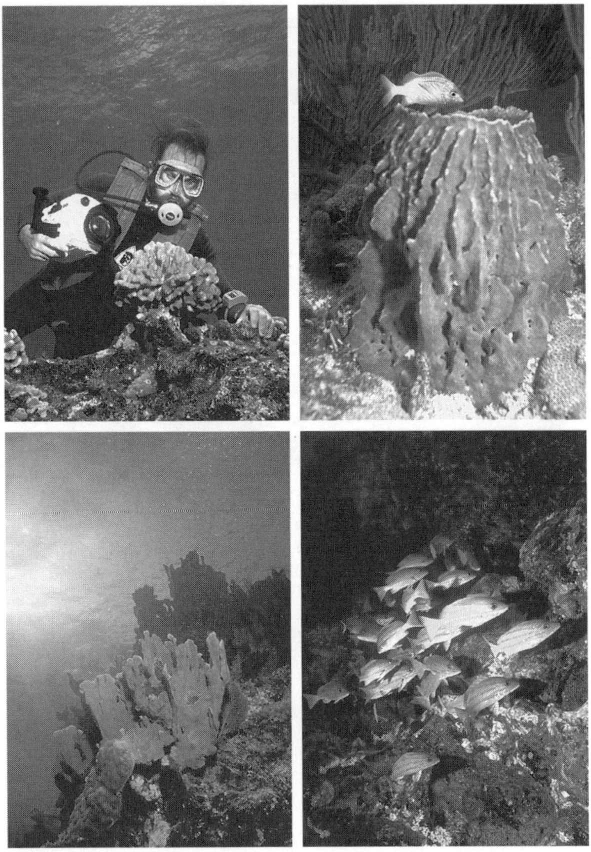

Figure 2-4 *The "standard" 28mm-35mm lenses found on most underwater cameras can still take a variety of interesting shots.*

■ Macro and Close-Up Shots Using Framers:

Many underwater camera systems allow you to attach extension tubes or external diopters with framers. This enables you to take what are known as *macro* or *close-up* shots. You will find more extensive information on macro and close-up photography in Chapter 5.

Typical macro and close-up subject matter includes: the textured surface of corals; sea fans and sponges; small crustaceans, such as arrow crabs; Christmas tree worms; and small, colorful shells, such as flamingo tongues (Figure 2-5). Be aware, however, that what this subject matter has in common is that *none of it is capable of moving particularly fast,* if at all. If your subjects could move with any speed, they would not likely choose to stand still long enough for you to surround them with a framer and take their picture.

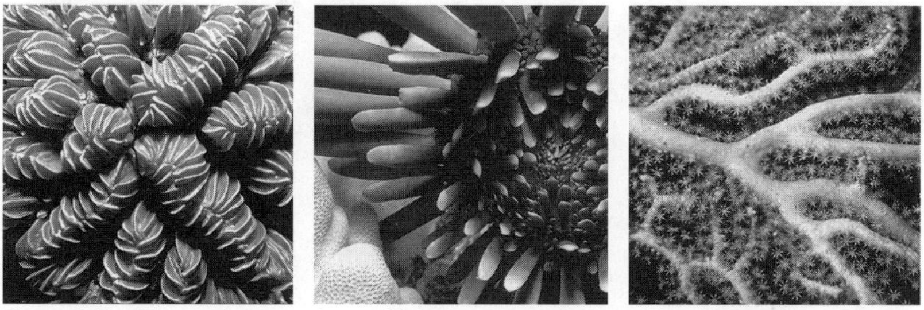

Figure 2-5 *Macro photography enables you to capture small but interesting subjects.*

- **Wide Angle Shots:** These are the shots you generally see on the covers of diving magazines and books. They cover a wide area and *appear* as though the photographer was 10-20 feet (3-6 metres) away when he or she took the shot (Figure 2-6). However, the fact that these pictures' primary subject matter is well lit and displays vivid colors tells us the photographer actually took the shot from no more than three to four feet (one to one-and-a-quarter metres) away. Obviously, this requires a special lens.

  Wide-angle lenses typically have a focal length of 15mm to 24mm. Their angle of coverage (technically known as *angle of acceptance*) can be up to 50 percent wider than what the human eye can see at the same distance.

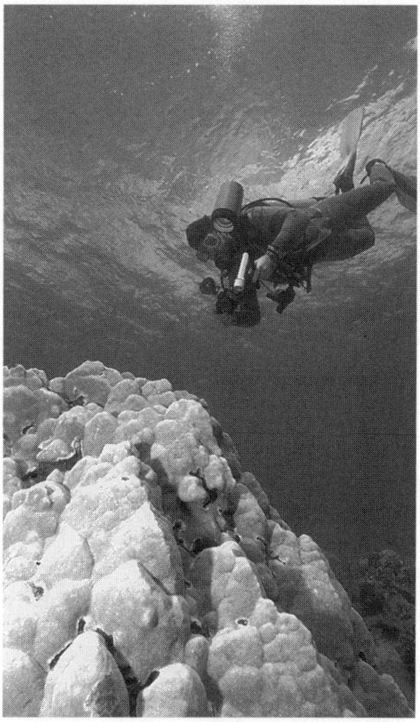

Figure 2-6 *Wide-angle lenses create the illusion that you took a picture from farther away than you really were.*

Wide-angle lenses capture some of diving's best and most dramatic photos. Photos of large aquatic creatures, such as whale sharks and manta rays, would not be possible without them. Wide-angle lenses are the primary tool of most professional underwater photographers. You will read more about wide-angle underwater photography in Chapter 5.

- **Silhouettes:** Although you will not want to spend all your time under water taking silhouette shots (Figure 2-7), you will undoubtedly want to have a few in your collection. The great thing about silhouette shots is that you can take them using almost any underwater camera and lens. You will learn how to take silhouette shots in Chapter 5.

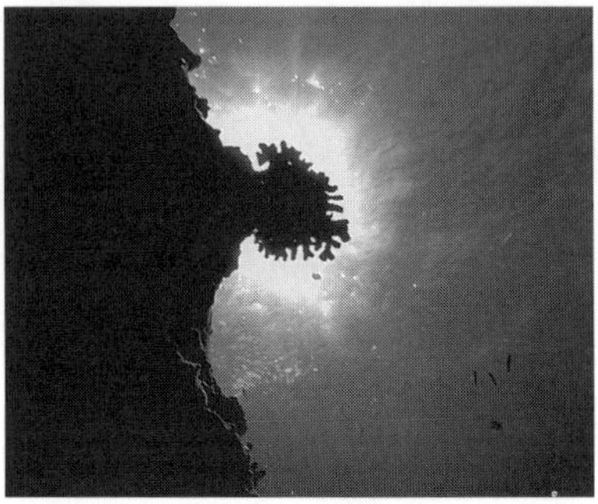

Figure 2-7 *Silhouette shot.*

- **Aquatic Animal Portraits:** At first glance, aquatic animal portraits (Figure 2-8) appear to be like any other type of macro or close-up photography. There is a critical difference, however. That difference is: *Few aquatic animals will remain still long enough for you to surround them with a macro framer, or even allow you to approach near enough to shoot them with an unframed, close-up lens.*

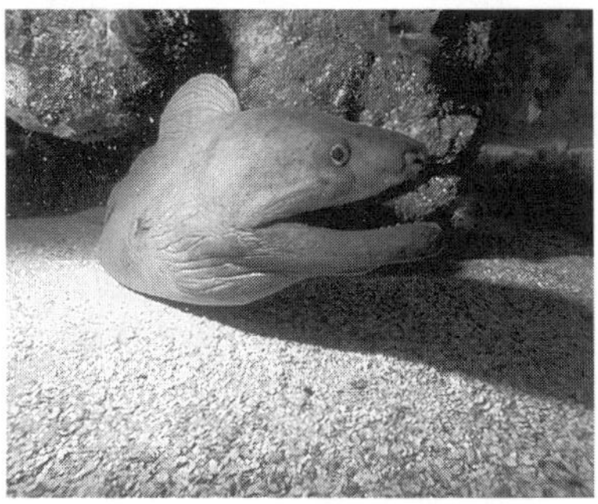

Figure 2-8 *Aquatic animal portrait taken with housed, Single-Lens Reflex (SLR) camera.*

  There are a few animals—noticeably angelfish—whom you can entice into your framer or into close-up lens range with food. Most likely, however, you will want pictures of more than just these few species. Additionally, feeding aquatic animals is seldom an environmentally sound activity.

  This means you need a different type of lens if you wish to shoot a wide variety of aquatic animal portraits. The consistent choice of professionals who shoot this type of picture is to use a *long-range* macro lens attached to a housed, Single-Lens-Reflex (SLR) camera. This type of system enables you to shoot aquatic animal portraits from far enough away that the animals are not generally spooked. You will learn more about this type of system shortly.

Selecting the Right Camera System to Meet Your Needs

Once you decide what types of underwater photos you wish to take, and prioritize which of these types of photos are more important to you, your next step is to find out which types of underwater camera systems will enable you to take these pictures.

This section describes the three basic types of underwater camera systems currently available. The chart in Figure 2-9 features the different types of underwater photos each system is capable of taking.

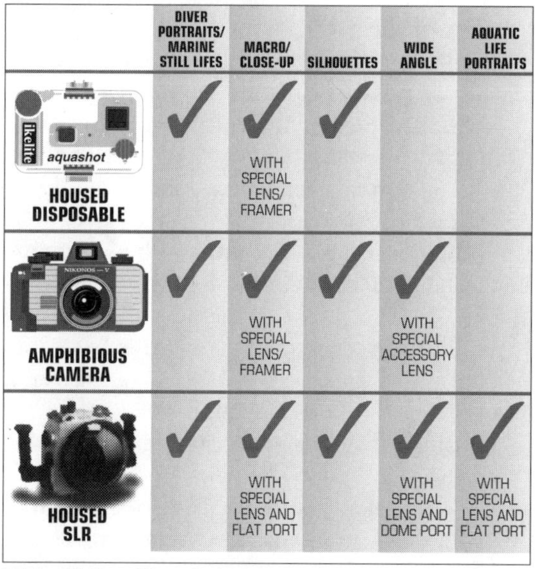

Figure 2-9 *All underwater camera systems can take a variety of shots. Not every system, however, is well suited to take every type of shot.*

Be aware, however, that this alone is not sufficient information upon which to base a sound buying decision. You should plan on having an in-depth discussion with your local SSI Dealer, who is in the best position to do a one-on-one assessment of your needs, and help you match those needs to the best available system.

- **Housed Disposable Cameras:** In the late 1980s, Kodak and Fuji both introduced a line of compact, disposable 35mm cameras. (The term *disposable* is not entirely accurate. When you bring the cameras in for processing, your photo lab and the manufacturer recycle the parts.) These cameras use highly-forgiving ISO 400 color print film, fixed-focus lenses and fixed apertures. The result are cameras that are both inexpensive and easy to use.

  Initially, Kodak and Fuji offered two versions of their disposable cameras, one of which came in a clear plastic, waterproof case. Unfortunately, these casings are only good to depths of less than 12 feet (3.7 metres). Additionally, these cameras rely on their own built-in flash, which has two limitations when used while scuba diving. First, these flashes are not powerful enough for use in any but very shallow water. Second, the built-in flash is right next to the camera lens. This creates a problem called *backscatter,* which you will learn about in Chapter 4 when we discuss strobe positioning.

Given these factors, it is relatively apparent the "waterproof" versions of these disposable cameras are, by themselves, better suited for snorkeling than diving. This does not mean, however, that you cannot take disposable cameras scuba diving.

Shortly after the introduction of disposable cameras, Ikelite and Fuji introduced re-usable housings that enabled divers to take these cameras to normal recreational diving depths. The Fuji version works only with Fuji disposables. As it still relies solely on the camera's built-in flash, it is better suited for snorkeling than diving.

The Ikelite Aquashot housing (Figure 2-10), on the other hand, is part of a series of available components that make it a full-fledged underwater camera system. The basic housing accommodates both Fuji and Kodak disposables. (The newer Aquashot II version accommodates the latest, 27-shot versions of these cameras.) Because the housing covers each camera's internal rangefinder, it also comes with an external, frame-style viewfinder.

Ikelite makes several accessories for the Aquashot. These include a water-correcting lens, an external strobe and a macro kit.

By themselves, the Kodak and Fuji disposable cameras focus best on objects six to ten feet (two to three metres) away. As you already know, the ideal range for taking pictures under water is no more than three to four feet (one to one-and-a-quarter metres). To compensate for this, Ikelite makes a *water-correcting* accessory lens (Figure 2-11) that enables the camera to focus on objects as close as 24 inches (60cm) away.

The Aquashot housing features a port through which the disposable camera's built-in flash can fire. As we covered previously, however, this flash is not powerful enough for underwater photos, and its position can cause backscatter problems. To overcome these limitations, Ikelite offers an external strobe (Figure 2-12).

Because disposable cameras have no internal electrical circuitry or sync-cord ports of their own, the strobe uses a slave sensor to trigger its flash. To use the strobe, you mount a special deflector plate over the flash port on the camera housing. This not only helps reduce backscatter caused by the internal flash, it deflects the flash's beam upwards and sideways, to where the slave sensor can most easily detect it, and fire the external strobe in sync with the camera shutter.

The macro kit includes a special framer, an external macro lens and a diffuser for the camera's built-in flash (Figure 2-13). It enables Aquashot users to take pictures of subjects roughly the size of a human hand.

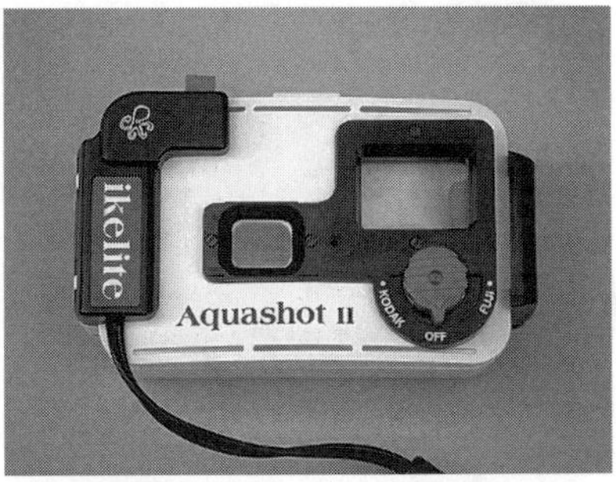

Figure 2-10 *Ikelite Aquashot II camera.*

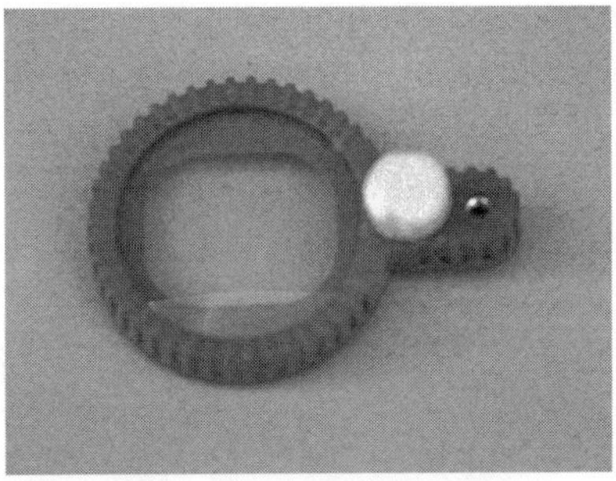

Figure 2-11 *The Aquashot's water-correcting lens enables the camera to focus on objects as close as 24 inches (60 centimetres) away.*

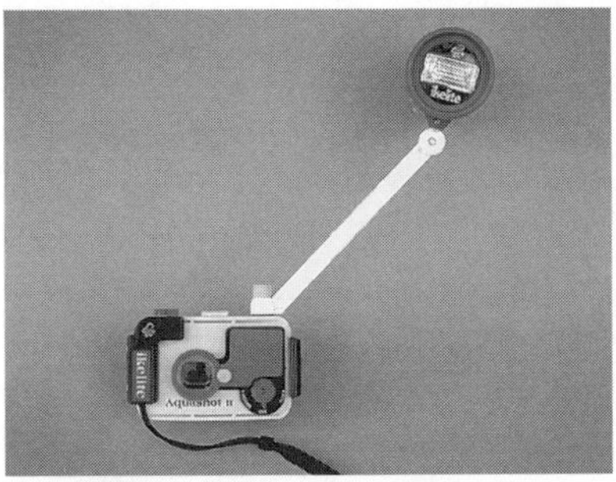

Figure 2-12 *External strobe and arm for Aquashot housing. Note the flash deflector used to reduce backscatter and direct the internal flash output to the strobe's slave sensor.*

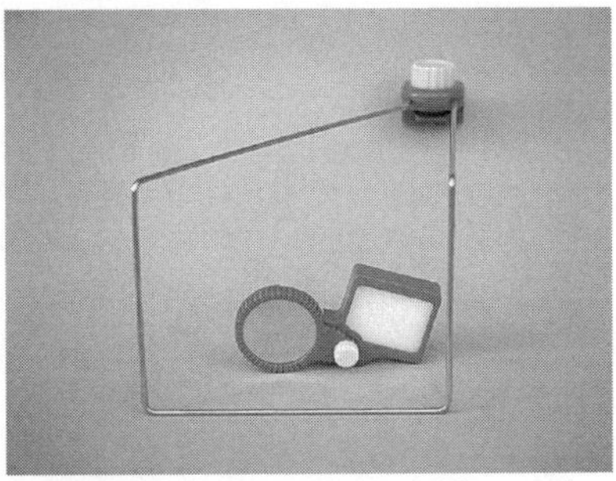

Figure 2-13 *Macro lens and framer for the Ikelite Aquashot.*

The chief benefit of the Ikelite Aquashot system is its extremely low cost. A complete Aquashot system, with all accessories, costs less than one-fourth of what most amphibious cameras or an SLR camera and housing does, once you add the cost of an external strobe to them.

In spite of its highly attractive cost, the Aquashot system has several limitations. Because it shoots only ISO 400 color print film, you will experience more graininess and less color saturation than you will with slower films. The lenses found in both disposable cameras and in the Aquashot housing itself are of nowhere near the quality of those in more expensive systems. This leads to further loss of detail in the resulting pictures.

Most dive resorts and boats or liveaboards can only develop slide film (Figure 2-14). This means that if you use an Aquashot, you will need to wait until you return home to see how well you did.

You must remember also that, with the Aquashot, you are limited to taking macro, silhouette, diver portrait and still-life photos. There are no accessories that will enable you to take wide-angle shots or extensive fish portrait work.

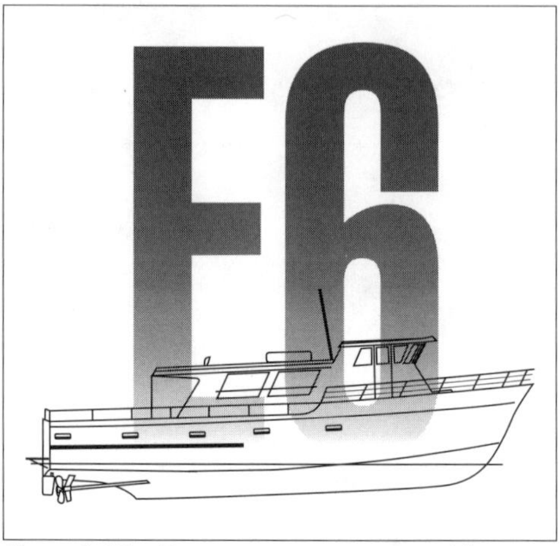

Figure 2-14 *Because most resorts and live-aboards can only develop slide film, you may have to wait until you return home to see how your disposable camera pictures turn out.*

Despite these limitations, the Aquashot represents an exceptional value for the money. It is inexpensive enough to be considered a true beginner's camera. Its low cost makes it a reasonable gamble for the diver who is not certain how much he or she will like underwater photography.

If you purchase an Aquashot and decide later to move up to a more expensive system, you will not have to abandon an investment in equipment you will no longer use. Once you purchase that more expensive system, you can loan the Aqua-shot to your buddy to use while you shoot your newer system (Figure 2-15).

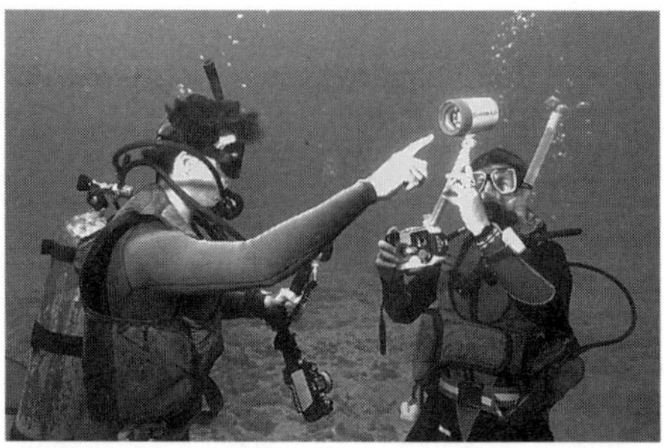

Figure 2-15 *If you later move up to a more expensive system, you can loan your Aquashot to your dive buddy.*

- **Amphibious Cameras:** Many manufacturers make waterproof cameras. Most of these cameras, however, are best suited for snorkeling. They suffer from many of the same depth and flash limitations as waterproof disposable cameras.

  Two manufacturers, however, make true underwater amphibious cameras: Nikon and Sea & Sea. We call these systems *amphibious* cameras because you can use them above and below water (Figure 2-16).

Sea & Sea's amphibious cameras include the MX-10, Motomarine II and Seamaster Pro. Nikon's current amphibious camera is the Nikonos V (the Nikonos RS, while technically an amphibious camera, has more features in common with housed SLRs, which we discuss next). All four cameras share several important features.

You can use most of these cameras above water with their standard 35mm lenses (Figure 2-17). You can also add accessory lenses to any of these amphibious cameras to take wide-angle and macro shots. In fact, the only type of photography for which these cameras are not well suited is extensive fish portraiture.

You can use these cameras' internal rangefinders or add external viewfinders. You can use any of these cameras, except the MX-10, with a wide variety of underwater strobes (the MX-10 uses a special, dedicated strobe). Both Nikonos and Sea & Sea cameras offer TTL strobe capability (Figure 2-18).

Amphibious camera systems are among the most compact underwater imaging systems you can use. This makes them easy to use in the water, and convenient to carry when traveling.

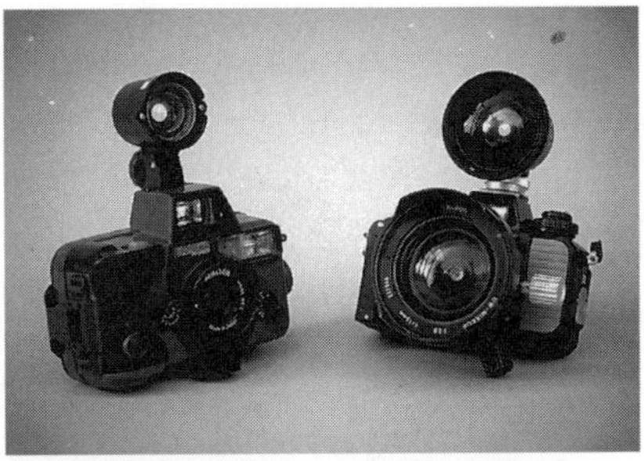

Figure 2-16 *Nikonos and Sea & Sea amphibious cameras.*

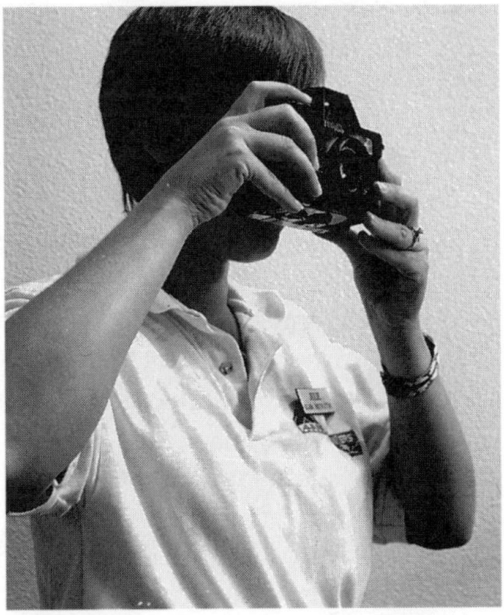

Figure 2-17 *You can use most amphibious cameras above water with their standard 35mm lenses.*

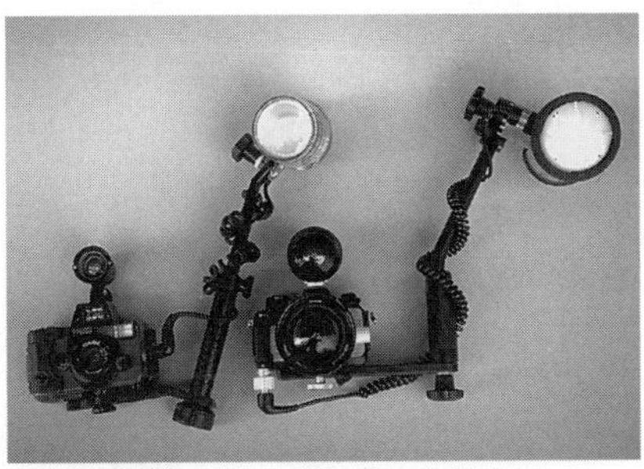

Figure 2-18 *Virtually all amphibious cameras offer TTL strobe capability.*

As with all systems, amphibious cameras have some drawbacks. Because you must use an internal rangefinder or external viewfinder, you run the risk of parallax error, discussed in Chapter 1. Additionally, to focus these cameras, you must estimate your distance to the subject. Because you do not look through the lens, as you do with SLR cameras, there is no way to confirm, for certain, that your subject is actually in focus.

Nevertheless, for many divers, the benefits of amphibious cameras far outweigh the drawbacks. They are, by far, the most popular underwater camera systems. Most of the photos you see in underwater magazines and books are taken with amphibious cameras.

- **Housed SLR Cameras:** Modern Single-Lens-Reflex (SLR) cameras are among the most sophisticated of all 35mm imaging systems (Figure 2-19). As you read in Chapter 1, SLR cameras offer the ability to compose photos by looking directly through the lens itself, thus eliminating the potential for parallax error. Today's 35mm SLR cameras offer other, highly advanced features that make them widely sought after photographic tools.

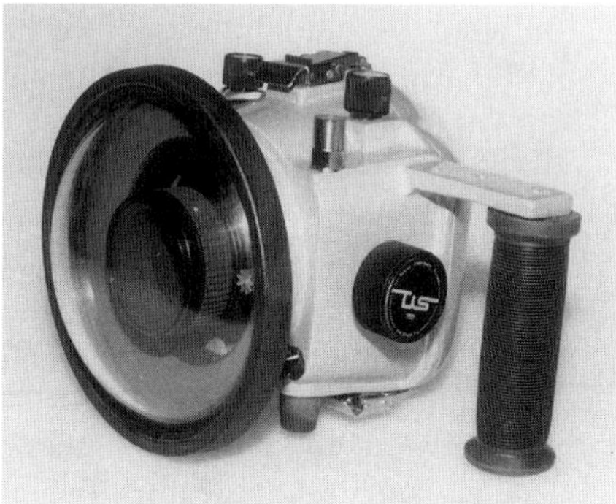

Figure 2-19 *Housed Single-Lens Reflex (SLR) camera system.*

Most current SLRs offer extremely accurate autofocus lenses. Many photographers consider them more accurate than the human eye. These lenses focus accurately in very low light, such as is common under water.

Autofocus lenses are particularly valuable when shooting SLR macro lenses. You may remember from our earlier discussion of the various types of underwater photos that there was no telephoto category. Given the drawbacks inherent in shooting through an unnecessarily long water column, this is not surprising. Nevertheless, SLR macro lenses share one feature with telephoto lenses: they have an extremely narrow depth of field (you will remember from Chapter 1 that this is the range in which subject matter will be in focus). So narrow is this depth of field that it is difficult for many photographers to keep macro subjects in focus unless they have the autofocus to help them (Figure 2-20).

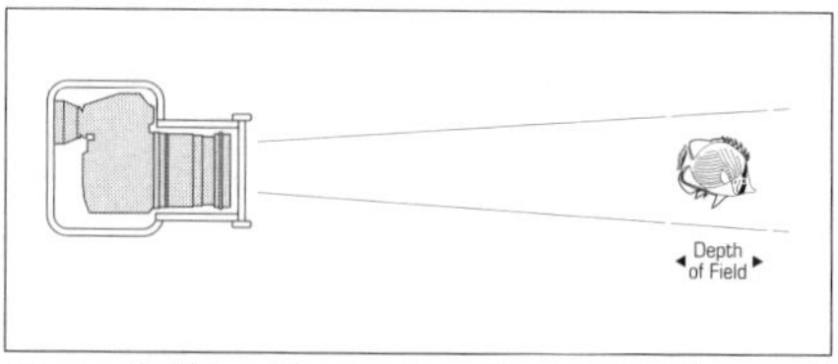

Figure 2-20 *The extremely narrow depth of field that SLR macro lenses provide makes autofocus an extremely valuable feature.*

Another feature modern SLR cameras offer is highly sophisticated metering systems. These systems are generally far more sophisticated than those found on amphibious cameras. Among the situations they can compensate for are ones in which lighting differs vastly throughout the lens's field of view (Figure 2-21).

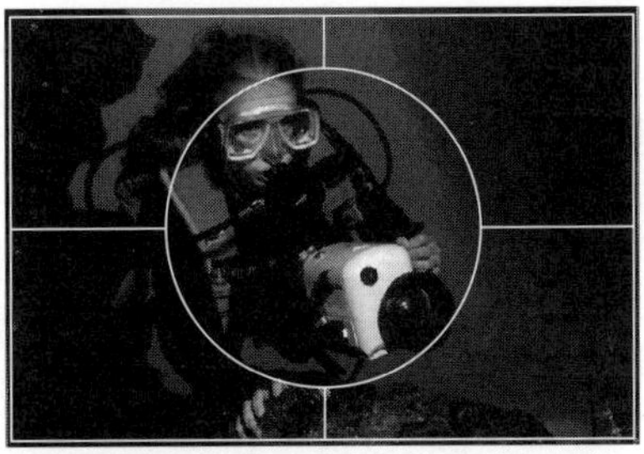

Figure 2-21 *The sophisticated matrix-metering system found on many modern SLR cameras can balance fill-in strobe illumination under widely varying lighting conditions.*

Given this wealth of features, it is not surprising that many photographers want to take their favorite SLR cameras under water. Fortunately, there are a variety of housings available that enable them to do so.

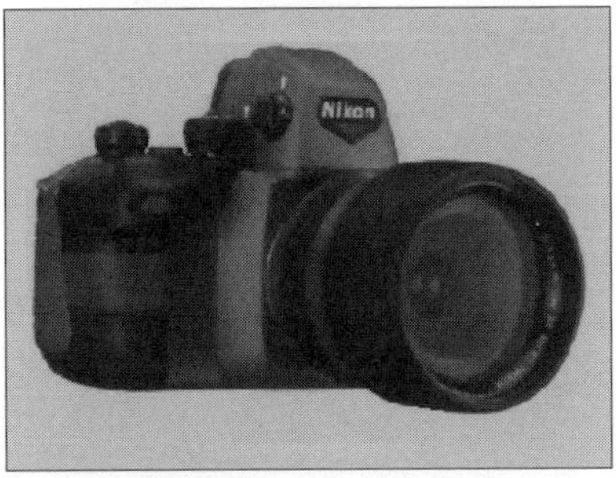

Figure 2-22 *Although technically an amphibious camera, the Nikonos RS is the functional equivalent of an advanced, housed SLR camera system.*

Housings are available for many of the most popular SLRs, including models from Nikon, Canon, Minolta and Pentax. An amphibious camera we mentioned earlier, the Nikonos RS (Figure 2-22), is really more like an SLR that comes with its own super-snug housing than it is like other amphibious cameras. Manufacturers generally fashion housings from rugged materials such as clear polycarbonates (Lexan®) or cast aluminum. This helps protect the more delicate equipment inside.

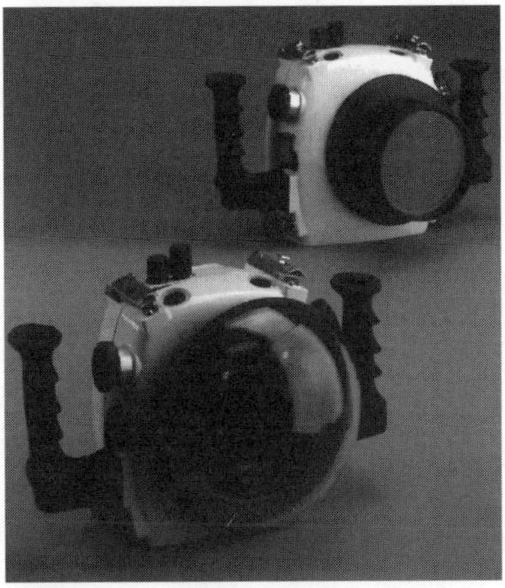

Figure 2-23 *SLR Camera housings equipped with dome (lower left) and flat (upper right) ports.*

Housing manufacturers offer a wide variety of interchangeable *ports* (Figure 2-23), so that housing owners can use a multitude of lenses with their systems. Flat ports accommodate long, macro lenses. Dome ports increase the effectiveness of wide-angle lenses, creating a *virtual image* in front of the lens which is nearly always in focus (Figure 2-24). The ability to use such a wide variety of lenses means that housed SLRs are the only system that can take every type of underwater photo discussed thus far. As an added benefit, if you invest in a housed SLR system, you also get an excellent topside camera to go with it.

Again, as with all systems, housed SLR cameras have their drawbacks. Chief among these is size and bulk. Using a housed SLR means moving a bigger object through the water, and overcoming more water resistance in the process. Housed SLRs are also more cumbersome to travel with.

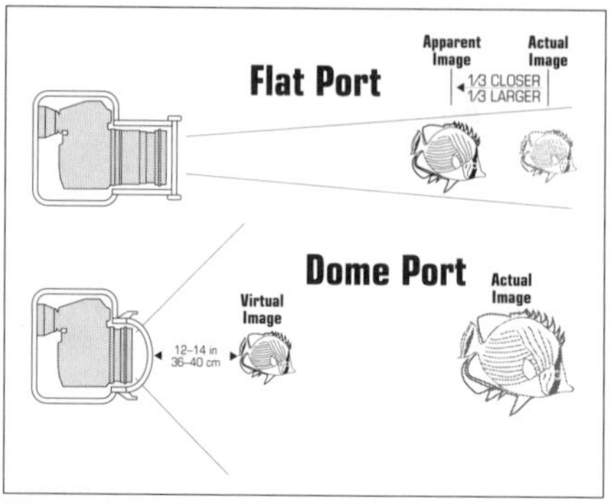

Figure 2-24 *Flat ports create an apparent image that is one-third closer and larger than the actual image. Dome ports create a virtual image in front of the camera's lens that is nearly always in focus.*

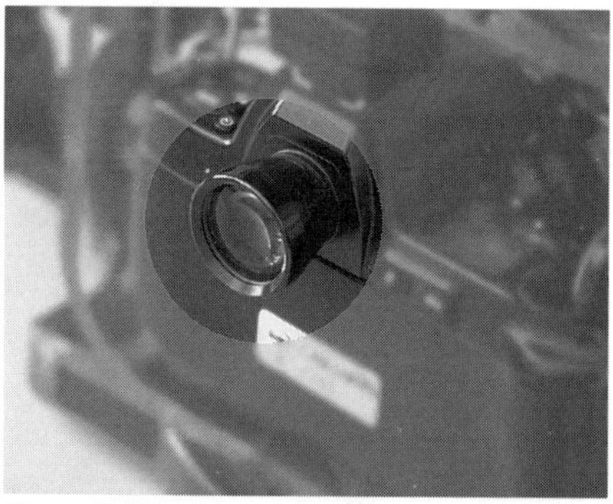

Figure 2-25 *Most housing manufacturers supply an eyepiece magnifier that makes it easier to see through the reflex viewfinder with a mask on.*

The benefit of being able to compose shots through the camera's lens is offset by the added distance the diver's mask and the housing create between the camera eyepiece and the diver's eye. Housing manufacturers overcome this limitation, to some degree, by including special *eyepiece magnifiers* with their housings (Figure 2-25). Professional series Nikon and Canon cameras are also available with extra-large *sportfinders* or *actionfinders*, that overcome this limitation entirely.

Some divers have a natural reluctance to take such a precision piece of mechanics and electronics under water, no matter how rugged the housing. Nevertheless, with proper care and maintenance, SLR housings should be every bit as reliable as amphibious cameras. Still, housing manufacturers recommend you take out a homeowner's or renter's insurance rider on your camera—just in case. This is not a bad idea with amphibious cameras, either.

The Importance of Artificial Light

When you first learned to dive, you also learned that water absorbs color. The deeper you go—and, consequently, the more water that light must pass through—the more color that water absorbs. Reds and yellow are the first colors to disappear. By the time light reaches depths approaching 100 feet (30 metres), the only colors left are blues and grays.

It is important for you to understand two more things regarding light and color absorption.

- **Ambient Light Loss:** First, as you descend, you not only lose color, you also experience a reduction in the *quantity* of ambient light. Depending on water clarity and time of day, you may lose up to half or more of the available light for every 33 feet (10 metres) you descend (Figure 2-26). In murky water, or earlier or later in the day, you lose even more light as you descend.

- **Direction of Travel:** The second thing you should understand is that light need not travel downward for absorption to occur. In ten feet (three metres) of water, the colors around you look much as they do at the surface. However, if you look horizontally at objects 100 feet (30 metres) away, they will appear in shades of blue and gray, much as they would if you examined them close up, at a depth of 100 feet. This is because as light travels horizontally through the water to your eyes, the water absorbs the same colors it would if that light had traveled 100 feet straight down (Figure 2-27).

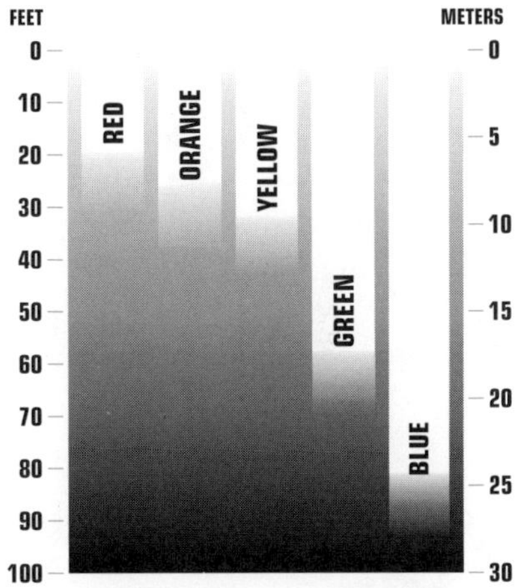

Figure 2-26 *Light and color absorption increase dramatically with depth; even in the clearest water, ambient light can decrease by 50% for every 33 feet (10 metres) of descent.*

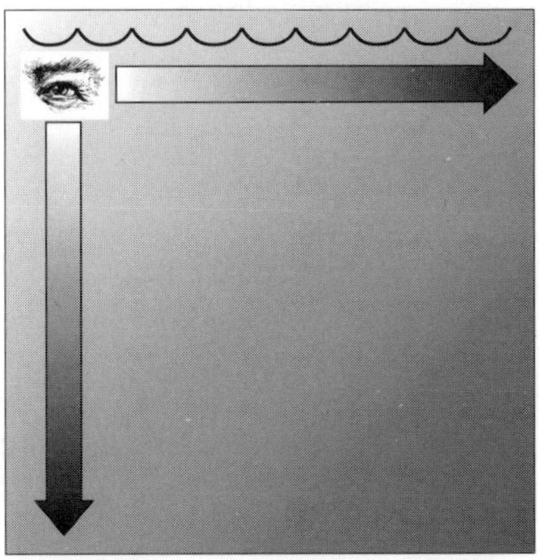

Figure 2-27 *Light and color absorption occur horizontally as well as vertically.*

How does light and color absorption impact our ability to take pictures? First, we must understand that our film is intended for use in daylight. Being under water is much like being indoors on a cloudy day. There simply is not enough light for film to perform well.

Thus, to have sufficient light to take good pictures—and, to make the colors in those pictures appear vivid and natural—we must use an artificial light source; an underwater strobe. As you gain experience in underwater photography, you will learn to make available light more of a factor in your photos. However, as a beginner, you will be highly dependent on your strobe for adequate lighting.

You should also understand that, because water is such a difficult medium to shoot through, the less water between you and your subject, the better pictures you will take. Conversely, if your subject is more than three to four feet (90 centimetres to 1.2 metres) away, only a tiny fraction of the light your strobe emits will actually hit the subject. By the time that light returns to your camera's lens, it will lose nearly all of its original intensity and color (Figure 2-28).

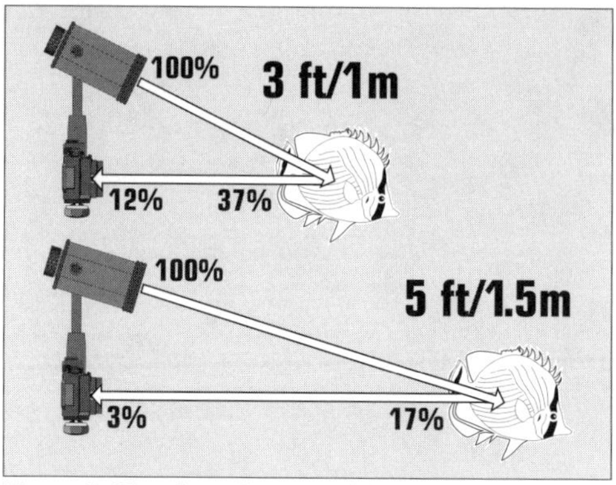

Figure 2-28 *At a distance of five feet (1.5 metres) from the camera, only a fourth as much strobe light returns to the camera's lens as occurs at a distance of three ft. (one metre). This is generally not enough strobe illumination to create pleasing pictures.*

Selecting the Right Film

If you select an amphibious or housed SLR camera, you will have a wide range of choices as to which film to use. Here are the factors you should take into consideration.

- **Speed:** Given the drastic reduction in ambient light that takes place below the surface, it is tempting to use the fastest film possible, to take advantage of its tremendous sensitivity to light. Remember, though, that higher speed films also mean a reduction in color saturation and detail (graininess). Vivid colors and sharp detail are among the chief reasons we take photos under water. Therefore, it makes sense to use the slowest film we can get away with, to maximize color and reduce grain.

Most underwater photo Instructors recommend their students begin with ISO 100 film. Over the years, ISO 100 film has proven to work well over a wide range of underwater conditions (Figure 2-29).

On overcast days, near dawn or dusk, or in deeper water, some photographers like to switch to ISO 200 film. This provides a good compromise between increased sensitivity to light and retention of color and detail.

Photographers who shoot extensively in wrecks or caves often use ISO 400 film (Figure 2-29). In these settings, color and detail are not as important. Increased sensitivity to light, however, is.

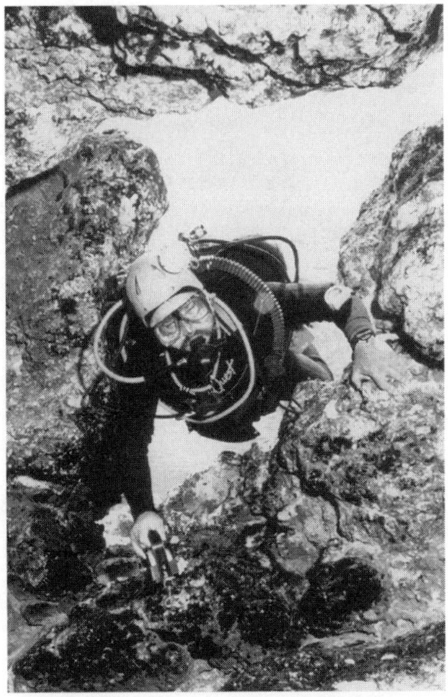

Figure 2-29 *Inside caverns and wrecks, faster films enable photographers to make maximum use of available and strobe light.*

Conversely, when shooting macro or close-up shots, the close proximity of the strobe to the subject matter means that light is not a problem. Similarly, in clear, shallow water, with the sun directly overhead, there may be plenty of available light. In these situations, many photographers choose to maximize color and detail by using ISO 64, ISO 50 or even ISO 25 film.

- **Type:** Which is better for underwater work, slide or print film? If you are shooting a disposable camera, or you want to shoot in black and white, you have no choice: You must use print film.

  What if you do not have these two limitations? Most serious photographers choose slide film over print film. At comparable film speeds, it generally offers better color saturation and finer grain. If you are shooting for publication, magazines generally prefer to receive transparencies rather than prints. Slide film costs less to develop. Finally, although it is more convenient to have enlargements made from color negatives, many photo experts believe that enlargements made from slides are of better quality.

  Despite the advantages slide film offers, many photographers still prefer to shoot print film. Usually this is simply because it is easier to show friends and family members a photo album than it is to set up a slide projector or viewer.

Print film also offers greater *latitude*—that is, it is more forgiving of mistakes in exposure. Many serious photographers do not consider this beneficial; it interferes with their ability to *bracket* photos (discussed in Chapter 5). Nevertheless, for beginning photographers who are still working to master exposure, this greater latitude may increase their chances of getting pleasing photos right away.

- **Developing:** Regardless of whether your long-term preference is for slide or print film, circumstances may dictate a temporary change. When shooting on a dive vacation, it is important you see the results of your work as soon as possible. This way, if an important shot does not turn out, you have a chance to retake it. If you find you need to change your photographic technique, you can make that change immediately. If your equipment is malfunctioning, it is important you discover this quickly and make any necessary repairs right way. If you wait until you get home to discover how your shots turn out, it will be too late to solve any of these problems.

  Most tropical dive resorts and liveaboards can only develop slide film that uses the E-6 process. Thus, when diving with these facilities, you will want to shoot slide film so that you can see the results of your work the next day. Conversely, at some destinations, such as Florida or Hawaii, it may be faster and more convenient to have prints developed. Before you travel, it is wise to find out what type of developing is available. This way you can make certain that the film you pack is the film you need.

CHAPTER 2 REVIEW

1. Many underwater camera systems allow you to attach extension tubes or external diopters with framers. This enables you to take what are known as ______________________________ ______________________________.

2. Wide-angle lenses typically have a focal length of 15mm to 24mm. Their angle of coverage can be up to 50% wider than ______________________________ ______________________________.

3. Because disposable cameras have no internal electrical circuitry or sync cord ports of their own, the strobe uses a ______________________________ to trigger its flash.

4. You can add accessory lenses to any amphibious camera to take ______________________________ and ____________________ shots.

5. Amphibious camera systems are among the most compact underwater imaging system you can use. This makes them easy to use in the water and convenient to carry ______________________________.

6. SLR cameras offer the ability to compose photos by ____ ____________________________ thus eliminating the potential for parrallax error.

7. SLR macro lenses share one feature with telephoto lenses: they have an extremely __________________ ____.

8. Depending on the water clarity and time of day, you may lose up to half or more of the available light for every ____________________ you descend.

9. If your subject is more than ____________________ ________________away, only a tiny fraction of the light your strobe emits will actually hit the subject.

10. Most underwater photo Instructors recommend their students begin with __________________ film.

Caring For Your Camera

3

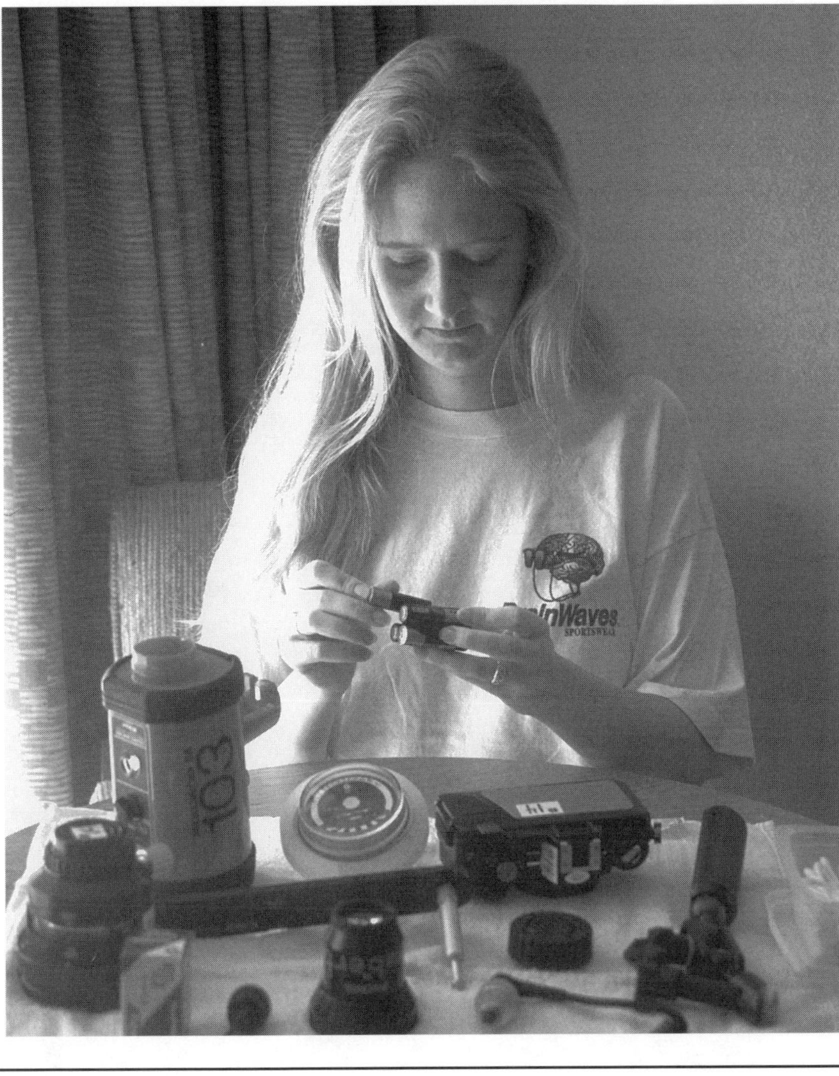

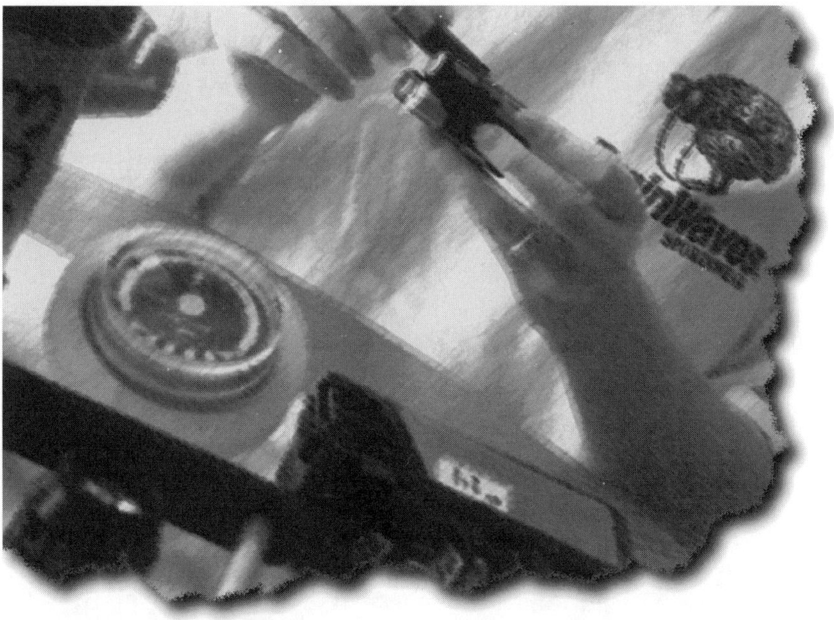

CHAPTER 3: CARING FOR YOUR CAMERA

Before you enter the water, there are steps you must take to protect your camera system from harm. When you exit the water, there are additional steps you must take that are equally important. These preventive maintenance procedures are more vital to the survival of underwater cameras than they are to any other type of still imaging system.

Additionally, if you do not set up your system correctly before using it, it will not only fail to work when you need it to, it may also be too late to solve the problem. For example, if you neglect to properly load film into your camera, by the time you return to the boat or shore, rinse and dry your camera system, then attempt to fix the problem, it may be too late to complete the dive.

Keep in mind as you read this chapter that we *are not* trying to scare you out of taking pictures before you start. Each year, thousands of divers shoot millions of pictures under water, without major problems. What these photographers have in common, however, is that they take the care and maintenance of their camera systems very seriously. You should, too.

THE MOST CHALLENGING ENVIRONMENT CAMERAS FACE

Modern cameras accomplish incredible feats. They scale mountains, withstand Arctic cold and bring back pictures of man's first steps on the moon. Yet these challenges are nothing compared to the rigors cameras face when we take them diving.

What No Topside Camera Ever Faces

When taking cameras under water, we ask them to face challenges that do not exist on land. Chief among these is the *force of water under pressure*.

The average land camera is mildly resistant to moisture. A short exposure to anything less than a downpour probably will not cause it much harm. Some land cameras are water *resistant*. If splashed, or even immersed in shallow water, their gaskets and seals will keep water out. However, once we take a camera system to normal, recreational diving depths, a force of up to *five times* the camera's internal pressure will attempt to drive this liquid—which is deadly to cameras—into their most vulnerable parts (Figure 3-1).

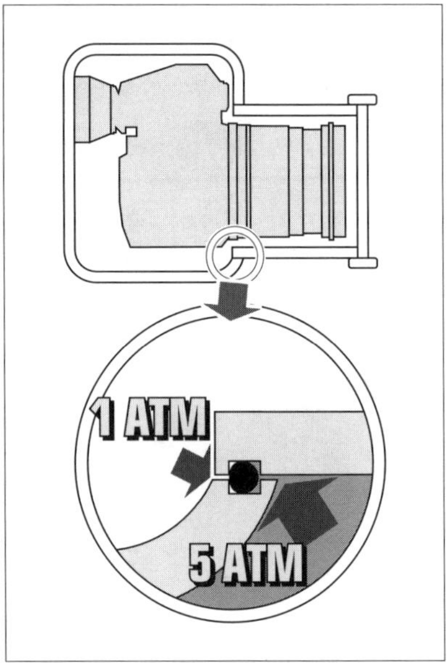

Figure 3-1 *Every time you dive, water tries to force its way inside your camera system at a pressure of up to five times greater than that inside.*

Make no mistake: Cameras do not react well to being flooded. Even the invasion of the purest fresh water will cause film to de-emulsify and batteries to leak corrosive acids. More often, however, the water that succeeds in entering underwater camera systems is anything but fresh. Water containing salt, electrolytes or ionized particles is particularly destructive to sensitive electronics and precision moving parts.

With prompt action, it may be possible to save a camera from the effects of a minor flooding. Usually, however, the camera is a total loss. Thus, the best way to deal with the possibility of camera flooding is to make certain it doesn't happen. That's what preventive maintenance is all about.

The Enemies That Attack After the Dive

Simply removing your camera from the water does not remove it from danger. Unless you dive in unusually pure, fresh water, your camera system's nooks, crannies, cracks and cervices will, after the dive, still contain water laced with salt, sand, minerals or sediment (Figure 3-2).

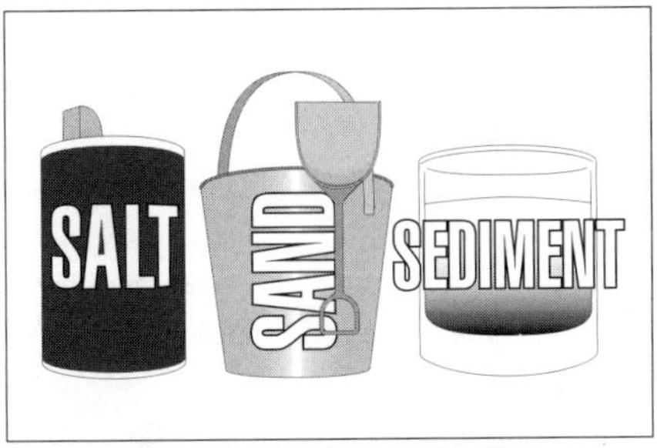

Figure 3-2 *After each dive, deadly agents will hide in your camera system's nooks and crannies unless you flush them out.*

Ironically, these contaminants are nowhere near the problem under water that they are on the surface. As long as they remain suspended in water, their potential for harm is minimal. However, when the water dries and these contaminants are left behind, trouble starts.

- **Salt:** This is the most dangerous contaminant. As salt dries, it forms razor-sharp, microscopic crystals that can damage O-rings and other delicate parts. Salt is a highly effective conductor of electricity. Moist salt crystals can cause an electrolytic reaction that seemingly dissolves aluminum casings and other metal parts. Salt build up can cement moving parts together as effectively as a weld.

- **Sand:** Ordinary beach sand can scratch lens surfaces. Wedged in cracks and crevices, it can carve water-conducting grooves in control shafts and file down precision parts until they no longer work.

- **Minerals and Sediment:** Just because you dive in fresh water does not mean you can stop worrying about the effects of contaminants on your camera system. If the water you dive in contains dissolved minerals and sediment, these contaminants can build up in cracks and crevices between dives. Among other damage, they can cement moving parts together as effectively as salt build up.

Rock and Roll

In some respects, taking a precision instrument, such as a camera, aboard a typical dive boat or to a typical beach site is like taking your fine china on a picnic...with a bull. The one is not ideally suited to withstand the rigors of the other.

Consider the following example. You accidentally drop your regulator on the deck. Big deal. Drop your underwater camera from the same height? You may not be so lucky.

Underwater camera systems are more susceptible to scratches, dings and impact damage than nearly any other dive equipment. They contain sensitive electronics, precision-ground lenses and delicate gearing mechanisms. Consequently, you must treat your camera system with even greater respect and care than your other equipment.

Adding to this challenge is the level of activity present at most dive sites. If you enter from a beach, you may encounter sand or mud that wants nothing more than to work itself inside the nooks and crannies of everything you own—including your underwater camera system. There may be breaking waves waiting to tumble you head over heels and, in the process, separate you from several hundred dollars worth of camera equipment.

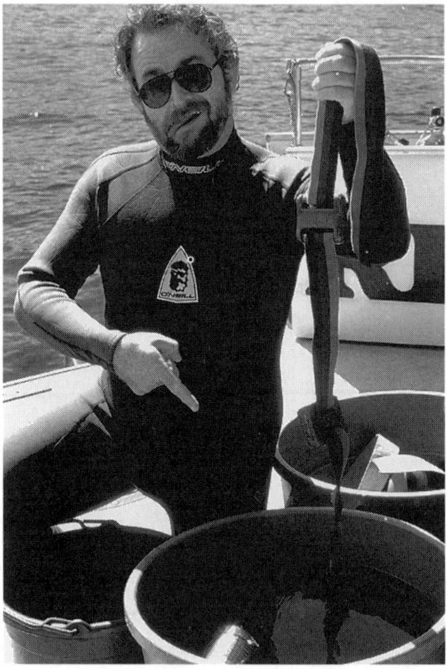

Figure 3-3 *"Okay if I rinse my weight belt in the camera bucket?" (You cannot count on other divers to understand how delicate your camera system is.)*

On dive boats, you will encounter fellow divers who have no idea how much you have invested in your camera system. Given the opportunity, they will sit on your camera bag, drop weight belts on top of your system while it is in the rinse bucket (Figure 3-3), or lean over the open back of your camera body with dripping hair, just as you are trying to change film. The fact that the boat deck is rocking back and forth like a mechanical bull will not help matters either.

Protecting Your Camera System From These Challenges

Given the threats posed by water under pressure, salt, sand, sediment, minerals, hostile dive sites and careless divers, your camera system depends on you for its very life. Take these challenges seriously—but don't let them intimidate you.

With a little conscientious effort, you can protect your camera system from damage and abuse. You will need to follow a regimen of careful pre- and post-dive camera maintenance, and have your system professionally serviced at least once every twelve months. You will also need to take special care transporting your system to and from dive sites, storing it on board dive boats and getting in and out of the water. Your reward for this effort will be a functional, reliable underwater camera system that gives you years of enjoyment and satisfaction.

PREPARING YOUR CAMERA FOR USE UNDER WATER

Taking your land camera out for a spin involves little more than popping in a roll of film, making sure the lens is clean and remembering to put in a fresh set of batteries when needed. Given the same level of inattention, your underwater camera system may die a rapid and painful death. You can help prevent its early demise by following some simple procedures each time your prepare your camera for use.

O-Rings: Your First Line of Defense

A considerable portion of preparing your camera system for use under water involves the removal, cleaning, inspection, lubrication and proper re-installation of O-rings.

- **What Are O-Rings?** An easy way to understand O-rings is to think of them as neoprene donuts. These donuts may be large or small; their cross sections may be thick or thin.

  Some camera housings may use a variation called an X-ring (Figure 3-4). A few older amphibious cameras may even have a gasket—similar, in many respects, to the one found underneath the valve cover on your car's engine—to seal the film door.

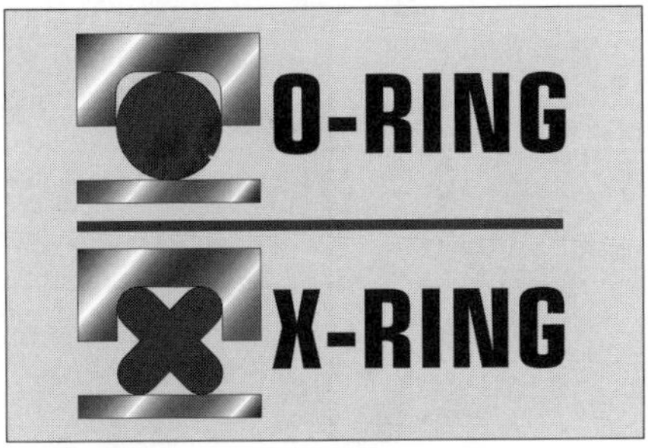

Figure 3-4 *X-rings work in a manner similar to O-rings.*

  Whatever its configuration, O-rings (and their close cousins, the X-ring and the gasket) serve one very important function. They guard the openings in your camera or housing from the invasion of water under pressure.

- **How Do O-Rings Work?** To work properly, O-rings must rest in some sort of groove. Both the O-ring and groove must be free of dirt and debris. Most important of all, the width of the groove must be narrower than the cross-section of the O-ring. This compresses the O-ring. In response, the O-ring presses against the sides of the groove with a pressure greater than that of the water trying to get past it. The result is that the water remains where it should, on the outside of the camera or housing (Figure 3-5).

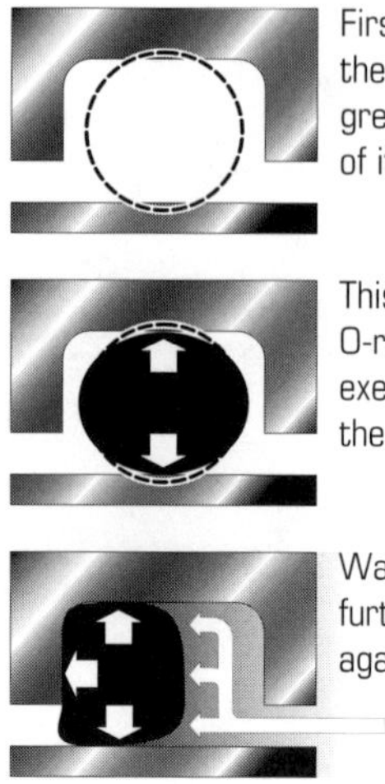

Figure 3-5 *How O-rings work.*

Four things can prevent O-rings from doing their job. Dirt particles or objects such as a human hair can force a section of the O-ring away from the side of its groove, creating a gap through which water can pass. Lack of lubrication can cause an O-ring to not seat properly in its groove, allowing water to pass. Some O-rings must be able to move inside their groove to function. Lack of lubrication interferes with this. Too much lubrication, on the other hand, can cause O-rings to slip out of their groove or attract dirt particles—either of which may cause O-ring failure. Finally, O-rings that are cracked, chipped or deformed in any manner may not be able to do their job, either.

■ **Basic O-Ring Preparation and Maintenance:** Each time you assemble your camera system or housing, you must perform a five-step process on each of its user-serviceable O-rings. These steps are: removal; cleaning; inspection; lubrication (if needed); and proper re-installation.

To perform these steps, you will need some basic supplies (see the accompanying article, *Creating a Maintenance Supply Checklist*). Chief among these are double-ended cotton swabs. You will need at least one cotton swab for every O-ring you service, plus spares. You will also need a tube or container of O-ring lubricant and some soft, lint-free paper towels. The lubricant you use should be one specifically intended for use with your underwater camera or housing. Do not use silicone spray.

Be aware that these items may not be readily available at dive resorts or on dive boats. Thus, when you travel, you should pack a supply sufficient for the duration of your trip.

Creating a Maintenance Supply Checklist

In reading this chapter, you've no doubt discovered that there is quite a number of other items that need to come along when you take your camera for a dive. A partial list of these items would include:

- Cotton swabs
- Lint-free paper towels
- Manufacturer-specified O-ring lubricant
- An eraser
- A medium-size coin
- A battery voltage tester
- Spare batteries
- Spare camera or housing O-rings
- Spare sync cord

This is just a beginning. Your personal system will undoubtedly require additional items.

Many divers like to add a small container of 1/4–20 stainless steel machine bolts in various lengths (1/2 inch being the most useful), with matching stainless steel nuts, flat washers and lock washers. This size bolt is commonly used to attach cameras, light meters and other mounting brackets to trays and arms. Of course, to use these items, you should bring along a standard, flat-bladed screwdriver and a small pair of pliers.

If you are a true pessimist, you'll bring along a container of de-ionized water, a small bottle of vinegar, a set of jeweler's screwdrivers and a hair dryer. These are the items you will need to deal with a flooding.

To pack all these items, look for a plastic container slightly larger than your camera or strobe. This way, when you reach your destination, your packing container can do double duty as a rinse tank.

The first step in O-ring maintenance is to remove the O-ring from its groove. Never use a sharp object to remove an O-ring. The preferred method is to squeeze the sides of the O-ring, so that a bulge appears, then push this bulge out of the groove with your free hand (Figure 3-6).

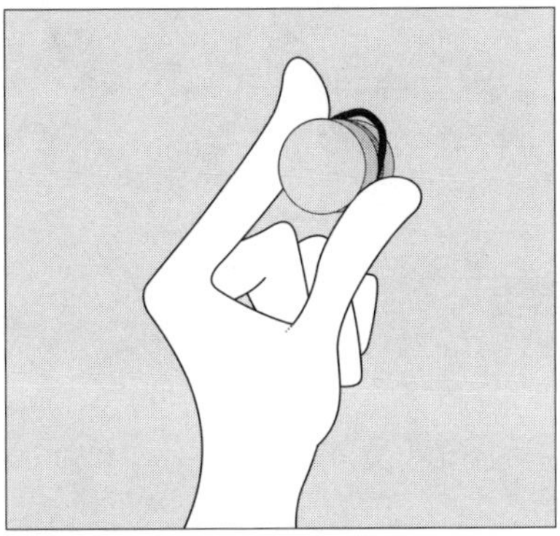

Figure 3-6 *The preferred method for removing O-rings is to not use sharp objects, but rather squeeze the O-ring out of its groove using just your fingers.*

With the O-ring removed from its groove, this is a good time to make certain the groove is free of dirt, neoprene particles and residual grease. Use one end of a cotton swab to clean the groove itself (Figure 3-7, page 52); use the other end to clean the seating surface opposite the groove where the edge of the O-ring will make contact (Figure 3-8, page 52).

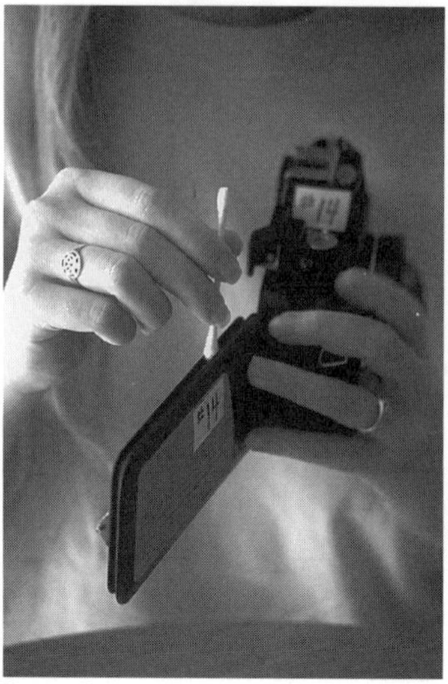

Figure 3-7 *Use one end of a cotton swab to clean the O-ring groove...*

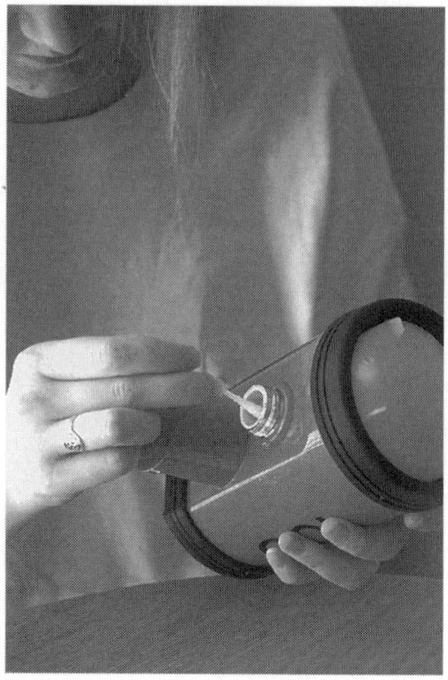

Figure 3-8 *...Use the other end to clean the seating surface.*

As you clean the groove and seating surface, twist and turn the cotton swab to make certain you are really removing potential contaminants, and not merely pushing them around (Figure 3-9). Use additional cotton swabs if needed to ensure these surfaces are truly clean. Once you have used a cotton swab to clean a groove or seating surface, discard it immediately to avoid the possibility of using it again.

The next step is to clean the O-ring so that no dirt, neoprene particles or excess lubrication remain. Thoroughly wiping the O-ring on a soft, clean paper towel usually suffices. If an O-ring is particularly dirty, you may wish to wash it in fresh, soapy water, then rinse and dry it thoroughly.

Once the O-ring is clean, you will need to inspect it. You should do this by examining the O-ring carefully with your eyes, and feeling its surface with your fingers. A magnifying glass helps. You may even be able to use one of your camera lenses for this.

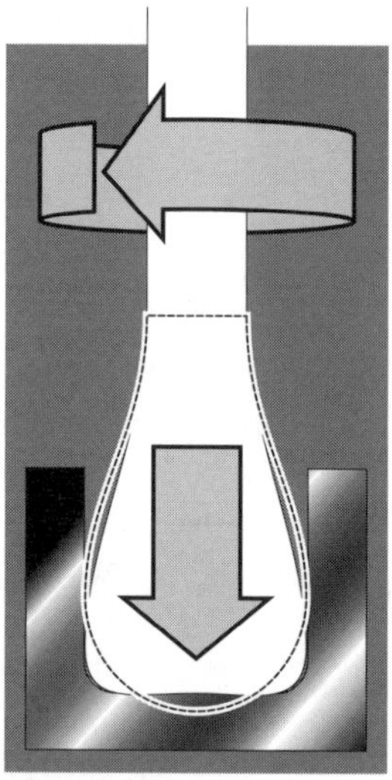

Figure 3-9 *Twist and turn your cotton swab as you clean each groove, making sure to push its tip all the way to the bottom; this helps ensure that you are not simply pushing dirt and grease around.*

What you are looking for when you inspect your O-rings are cuts, cracks, nicks or deformities (Figure 3-10). The presence of any one of these means the affected O-ring should be replaced. Of course, to be able to do this, you are going to have to carry a complete replacement set of O-rings with you.

Once you have removed, cleaned and inspected an O-ring, and cleaned the groove in which it will rest, the next step is to determine if it needs additional lubrication. A properly lubricated O-ring has a smooth, uniformly shiny surface. A dull, flat-looking surface indicates insufficient lubrication. A visible layer of grease, on the other hand, indicates too much lubrication.

To lubricate a smaller O-ring, place a tiny dab of O-ring lubricant on the tip of your index finger. Place the O-ring on this finger and use it and your thumb to work the grease into all exposed O-ring surfaces. To lubricate a larger O-ring, place the grease in the valley formed by one of your index finger joints. Move the entire circumference of the O-ring through this joint while working the lubricant in with your thumb (Figure 3-11).

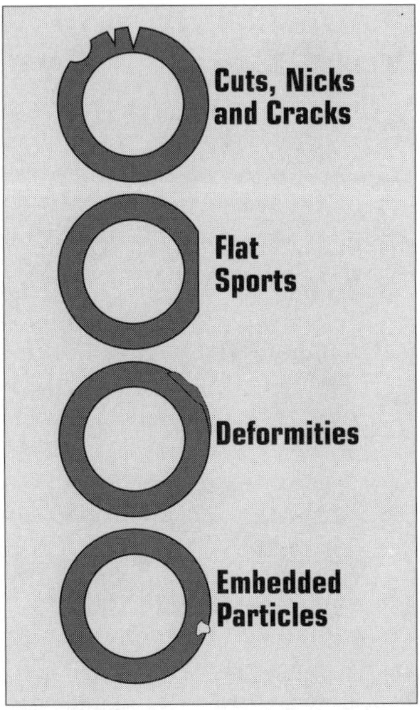

Figure 3-10 *Inspect each O-ring carefully to detect the presence of problems such as these.*

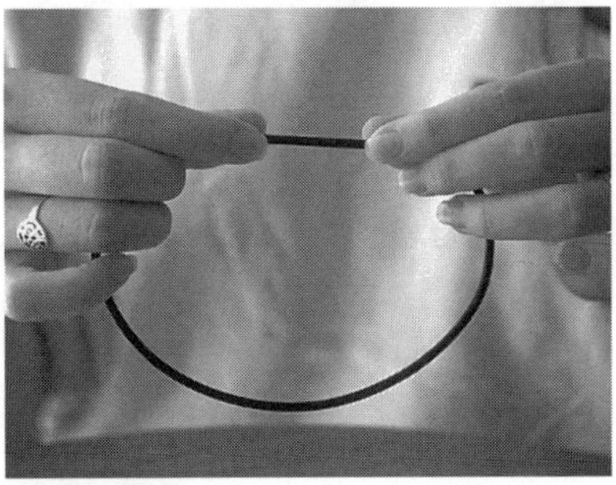

Figure 3-11 *Technique for lubricating large O-rings.*

When finished, wipe any excess grease off the O-ring with a soft, clean, lint-free paper towel. Feel the O-ring once more with your fingers. If you detect any grit, wipe the O-ring clean and repeat the lubrication process again.

Once you have lubricated an O-ring, re-install it in your camera system immediately. Leaving a lubricated O-ring exposed to air can attract dust, sand and other unwanted particles.

Assembling and Testing Your Camera System

Before you use your camera system under water, you must first assemble and test it. To better understand the steps involved, it helps to first explain the steps you should follow when you finish using your system. We will cover these steps in detail later on in this chapter; however, here is a brief overview.

> *After thoroughly rinsing and drying your camera system, you will disassemble all its component pieces for storage. This will include removing the batteries from your strobe and—assuming you have one—your amphibious camera body. You will also disconnect the sync cord from both your strobe and the camera body or housing. You will further take apart the strobe arm, tray and any other accessories. With everything disassembled, you will store all the camera-system components in a dust- and moisture-proof container.*

Now, when you want to use these items again, you will need to reassemble and test them before taking them in the water. The exact procedures to follow will vary, depending on your system. Consult your owner's manuals and your SSI Dealer or Instructor for recommendations to follow with your particular camera or housing and strobe.

In the paragraphs that follow, we've listed the main steps common to most systems. You will undoubtedly want to work through these steps the first time with your SSI Underwater Photography Instructor or the camera expert at your local SSI Dealer.

- **Select the Best Spot to Assemble Your System:** At the beach or on board a dive boat is no place to be setting up your camera system. Blowing sand, salt spray, rocking decks and jostling by dripping wet divers make these very poor places to perform critical pre-dive assembly and testing procedures. Underwater camera assembly is something that should take place indoors, away from as much dust, sand, moisture and traffic as possible.

  If you will be shooting pictures locally, the ideal time to assemble your camera system is before you leave home. If you are on vacation, you should assemble your system in your hotel room, prior to leaving for the boat (Figure 3-12).

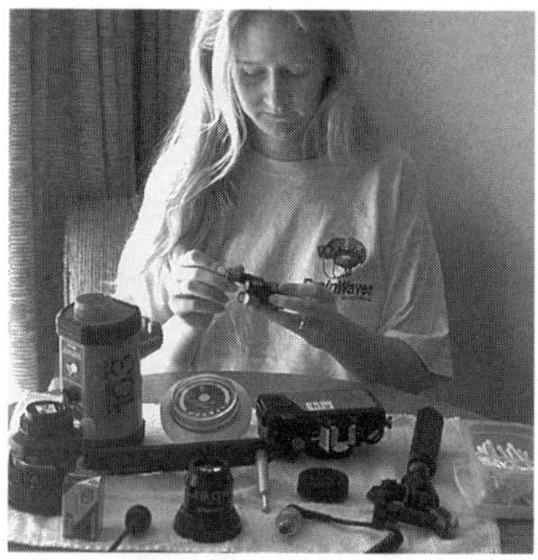

Figure 3-12 *Completely assemble and test your camera system before leaving for the dive site.*

(Note: Due to their large size, stable decks and spacious interior accommodations, we'll assume that being on board most liveaboard dive vessels is as good as being in a hotel room or at home. Besides, once at sea, where else are you going to go?)

What About Changing Film On Board?

Throughout this chapter we emphasize the importance of assembling and loading your camera system before you leave for the dive site or boat, and of disassembling it only after you return to your home or hotel room. The reason is that the typical dive boat or dive site is a poor place to have the inside of your camera system open and exposed. The blowing sand, salt spray and dripping divers one finds on dive boats and at beaches is not good for your camera's health. Additionally, it's tough to do a good job of servicing O-rings or doing similar procedures under these conditions—especially on a rocking boat. You can easily understand, then, why it is a good idea to avoid changing film on board a dive boat or at the beach.

You may be able to avoid this need by using 36-exposure film. Many new divers have difficulty shooting more than 20 exposures on a single dive. By dividing a 36-exposure roll of film between two dives, you may eliminate the need to change film—without feeling that you have missed any great photo opportunities on either dive.

Sooner or later, however, you will find yourself having to change film on a boat or at the beach. When this happens, here are some steps you should take.

- *Rinse your camera system as thoroughly as possible before you start.*
- *While allowing the system to dry, strip off the upper portion of your wet suit or dive skin. If it is a full-length suit, pull it down to the waist and tie the arms behind you. Use a towel to dry your upper body and hair as thoroughly as possible.*
- *Towel any remaining moisture from your camera system, then move it, your film and your maintenance supplies to the most protected area possible. At the beach, this will likely be inside a vehicle. On a boat, this will be inside a well-protected cabin—and as far away from diver traffic as you can get. Stay out of direct sunlight, but have enough light so that you can clearly see what you are doing.*
- *When opening the film compartment door, point it downward. This way, any trapped moisture will tend to fall out of the camera, rather than farther inside.*
- *Re-load following the procedures outlined earlier in this chapter. Be particularly careful to make sure no loose, wet human hairs end up between an O-ring and its groove.*
- *Test your system in the rinse bucket before taking it back in the water.*

Changing film on board an open, rocking boat or on a sandy beach is not ideal. However, by following these procedures, you can eliminate some of the potential for problems.

- **Load and Test Your Strobe:** This is a good place to start. Load alkaline or rechargeable batteries into your strobe. There will usually be a diagram to help you insert the batteries the right way. If your strobe comes with a rechargeable battery pack, charge the pack completely, according to the directions.

  Just before inserting a battery, use an ordinary eraser on each of its ends. This will remove grease and corrosion and help ensure a solid electrical contact.

  The cap or door that seals the battery compartment will have an O-ring. Service this O-ring following the procedures outlined earlier. Be aware that on some Ikelite strobes, the battery door O-ring is glued in place. Do not try to remove this O-ring; simply clean, inspect and—if necessary—lubricate its exposed surface.

  Once you have loaded the batteries, turn the strobe's power switch to the *on* position. If this or another switch controls the level of strobe power output, make certain it is set for *full power*. The *ready light* should glow at full intensity within a period of time specified in the owner's manual—usually six to ten seconds. The ready light indicates that the strobe's capacitors are fully charged and ready to power the flash tube. (Figure 3-13).

  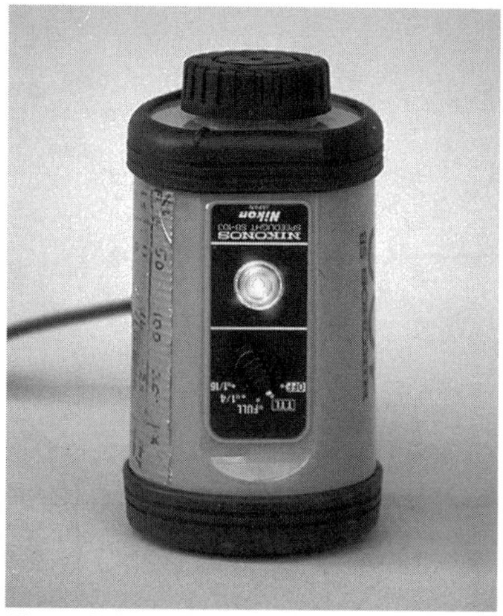

  Figure 3-13 *The ready light indicates your strobe's capacitors are fully charged and ready to power the flash tube.*

  If it takes longer than ten seconds for the ready light to fully illuminate, your batteries may need replacing. If you have one, you can use a battery voltage tester to see if your alkaline batteries are still usable or your rechargeable batteries are fully charged.

  Some strobes enable you to test fire them independently of the camera. If your strobe allows this, do so. There should be a bright flash of light, after which the strobe should fully recycle (that is, the ready light returns to full intensity) within six to ten seconds, or less.

- **Connect Your Strobe and Test Your TTL Circuitry:** Assuming everything with your strobe appears in order (and you are shooting something other than a housed disposable), the next step is to connect the sync cord to your strobe on one end, and to the camera or housing on the other.

You will most likely have O-rings to service on each end of the sync cord (a few sync cords are permanently attached to the strobe on one end). As you service these O-rings, be careful not to get O-ring grease on the electrical connections. As a precaution, it is a good idea to clean these contacts with your pencil eraser just before inserting them in the camera body, housing or strobe.

Your sync cord connections will be indexed, to help prevent you from inserting them incorrectly (Figure 3-14). Locate these before you plug in either end of the sync cord. As you insert sync cord connectors into your camera or strobe, be very careful not to twist the tiny pins on either end. Doing so could require a costly repair.

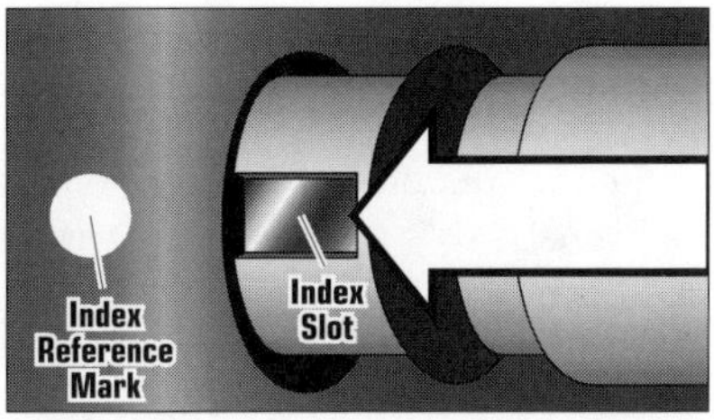

Figure 3-14 *Your sync cord connector will be indexed, to help you insert it the right way.*

If you are shooting an amphibious camera, clean and insert its batteries at this time, making certain to orient them correctly. There will be a battery compartment O-ring to service when you do so. If you are shooting a housed SLR, connect your housing's internal hot-shoe plate or PC connector to the camera body.

Now you are ready to test your camera system's ability to fire the strobe. Without loading any film, advance your camera's film counter to the first frame.

If your system does not have TTL strobe capability, simply switch your strobe to the *full power* position, wait for the ready light to fully illuminate, then depress the camera's shutter release while pointing the strobe away from you. There should be a bright discharge of strobe light, after which the strobe should recycle in approximately the same amount of time it first took for the ready light to come on.

If your strobe fails to fire, re-check your sync cord connections and try again. If the strobe still fails to fire, a faulty sync cord is generally the culprit. Replace the cord and try a third time. If this fails to solve the problem, it is time to seek professional service.

If your camera system has TTL strobe capability, turn your strobe to the *TTL* position and wait for the ready light to fully illuminate. Now look in the camera's internal viewfinder and depress the shutter release slightly. You should see a confirmation signal indicating that the camera believes the TTL circuitry to be connected (Figure 3-15, page 58). Your camera owner's manual will tell you what this confirmation signal will look like.

Next, open the aperture to its widest setting. Hold the camera so that the front faces you and aim your strobe directly into the lens

(Figure 3-16). Depress the shutter. There should be a brief flash. The strobe's ready light should wink momentarily, if at all, then quickly return to full intensity.

This test confirms that the camera's TTL circuitry can successfully shut the strobe off as soon as the sensor registers that sufficient light has entered the camera. In this test, because of the close proximity of the strobe to the lens' wide-open aperture, the strobe must discharge only a tiny fraction of its total capacity to activate the TTL sensor. Because this results in only a minute discharge of the strobe's capacitors, the ready light should only dim momentarily. This dimming may not even be detectable.

If your TTL strobe fails to fire or, if it fires but a blinking ready light or long recycle time indicates that the strobe fully discharged, you have a problem. Try the corrective procedures previously outlined for non-TTL strobes.

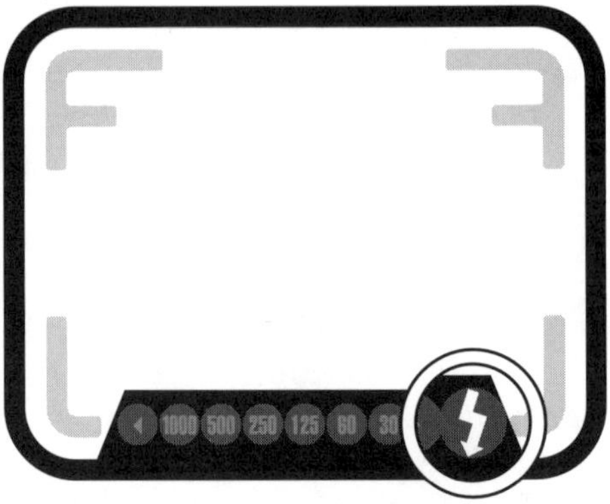

Figure 3-15 *One way you can tell your TTL circuitry is functioning properly may be a confirmation signal in the camera's viewfinder.*

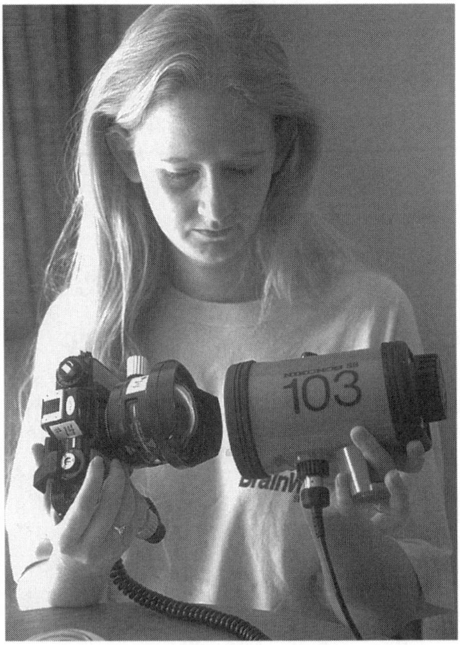

Figure 3-16 *Testing TTL strobe function.*

- **Attach or Service Your Lens or Port:** After installing batteries in your camera and strobe, connecting the sync cord and testing all associated circuitry, the next logical step is to service your lens or housing port. If you have a Sea & Sea camera or Ikelite Aquashot housing, you get to skip this step. These units have built-in lenses that do not require service.

If you are using any model Nikonos camera, you will need to either install the right lens or lens/extension tube combination, or at least service the O-ring of the lens that is already in place. If you are shooting a housed SLR camera, you need to either install the right lens port or service the O-ring of the lens port that is already on the housing.

Exact procedures for installing lenses or ports may differ. One thing each task has in common is that you will need to follow the basic O-ring maintenance procedures outlined previously.

As you work with the appropriate lens or port, take care not to get O-ring grease, fingerprints or dirt on lens elements or port surfaces. If you do, you can clean these items with special lens tissues and cleaning solutions. Be aware, however, that even if you follow the manufacturer's recommendations for cleaning lenses and ports, you still run the risk of causing a minor amount of damage. If it isn't dirty, don't clean it.

The best way to keep lenses and ports clean is to avoid getting them dirty. Keep the lens cap or dome port cover in place unless you are testing the strobe or getting ready to enter the water (Figure 3-17). Don't be concerned about minor dirt or water spotting on the exterior of lenses or ports—this will dissolve as soon as you go under water.

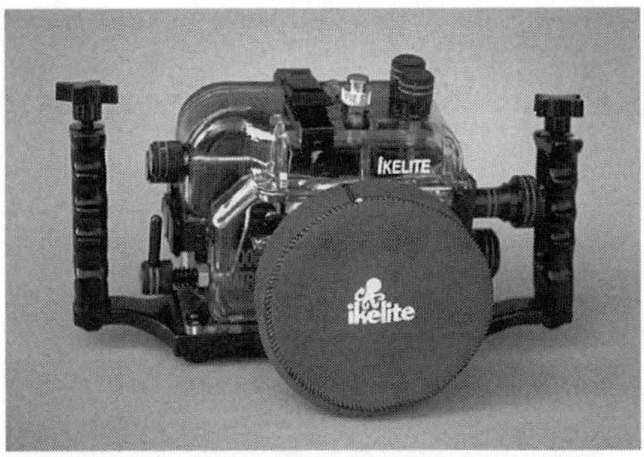

Figure 3-17 *To protect your lens, keep the dome port cover or lens cap in place until you are ready to enter the water.*

- **Load Film and Seal the System:** Among the final steps in preparing your camera system is to load film into the camera and to seal the film door or housing back.

  Exact film loading procedures vary widely from camera to camera. You will need to consult your owner's manual, a book dedicated solely to your camera system or—better still—a staff member at your local SSI Dealer who is familiar with your system. Some cameras load film automatically. Others require several intricate steps. Whatever system you have, be patient. There is nothing to gain by rushing.

  If your camera has a manual advance, extend the rewind crank and remove any slack from the film before advancing the film to the first frame. (Make certain first, however, that the camera is not in its rewind mode.) As you advânce toward the first frame, the rewind crank should spin (Figure 3-18, page 60). This confirms that the take-up spool is, indeed, winding film. Many underwater photographers have missed once-in-a-lifetime shots because they thought they had correctly inserted their film leader into the take-up spool—but did not bother to check it.

If you are shooting an amphibious camera, load your film before you service the film door O-ring. If you service this O-ring first, its lubricated surface may attract dust particles while you load the film.

If you are shooting an amphibious camera, close and seal the film door before advancing to the first frame. If you are shooting a housed SLR, advance to the first frame before sealing your housing.

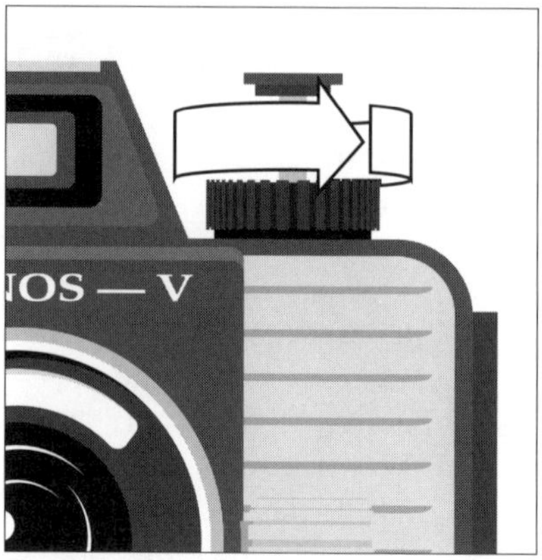

Figure 3-18 *To make sure your take-up spool is actually winding film, some cameras allow you to extend and watch the rewind crank advance.*

- **Mount Trays and Arms:** The very last step in your assembly procedure is to attach your system's mounting trays and arms. One common trick here is to wrap the sync cord loosely around the strobe arm. This reduces the possibility of the cord accidentally getting in front of your lens and ruining a shot (Figure 3-19).

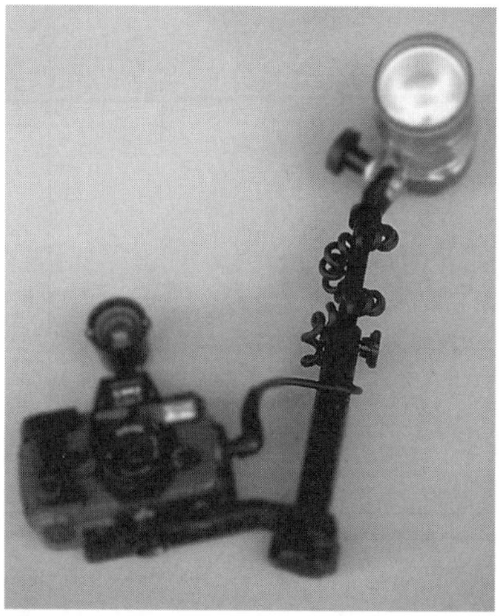

Figure 3-19 *Wrapping the sync cord around the strobe arm will help prevent it from accidentally getting in front of the lens.*

- **Test Your System's Integrity:** Before leaving for the dive site, immerse your system in a container or tub of fresh water. There will be a small quantity of air trapped in handles, arms and elsewhere that may take a few seconds to dislodge itself from your system and float to the surface. Tapping your system gently with a finger will help dislodge bubbles trapped in cracks and crevices. A steady stream of bubbles continuing to flow after more than a few seconds is a sign of trouble. Re-check the O-rings in the indicated area before taking your system under water.

Transporting Your System To and From the Dive Site

Simply being transported to and from dive sites can be hazardous to your camera system's health. Unprotected camera systems can be dropped, sat on, banged up or stolen. You really have two areas of concern here. First, how will you protect your system while transporting it long distances, *disassembled,* such as when flying to a tropical resort destination? Second, how will you transport your *assembled* camera system from your home or hotel room to the dive site or boat?

- **Long Distance Protection:** The best way to protect your unassembled camera system when traveling long distances is to use a special protective case. The most common of these are made from hard plastic or aluminum.

  Inside, these cases will have foam-padded dividers or die-cut ("pick and pluck") foam cubes. If you choose a case with dividers, you will find you can configure them into a variety of different-size compartments. Die-cut foam cubes can be selectively removed to create custom-fitted spaces for each individual system component.

  Additional features common to this type of case include: O-ring seals to keep moisture out; venting screws to equalize internal pressure after flying; and padlock holes to help prevent tampering.

- **Getting To and From the Dive Site or Boat:** Once you assemble your camera system, you will need a safe and secure way to transport it to and from your home or hotel room and the dive site or boat. Simply throwing it in your gear bag is out of the question.

  If your camera system is small, you may be able to simply hand carry it. If you own the type of hard-sided carrying case with removable dividers, you may be able to take these dividers out and transport your system to the water this way. If neither of these are options, ask the underwater photo expert at your SSI Dealer for his or her suggestions on creating a suitable carrying container.

Protecting Your Camera System On Board Dive Boats

If you will be diving from a boat, ask the crew as soon as you board where the best and safest place to store camera systems is. They may have a special shelf or table for this (Figure 3-20).

If the crew has no suggestions, you may have to look for the best place on your own. What you are looking for is anywhere the camera is not likely to be sat on, stepped on, have equipment dropped on it, bounce up and down on the deck or wash overboard. This area should also be out of direct sunlight.

If you have to, be prepared to keep the camera system with you at all times. Fortunately, given the increasing popularity of underwater photography, most modern dive boats are built to accommodate photographers' needs.

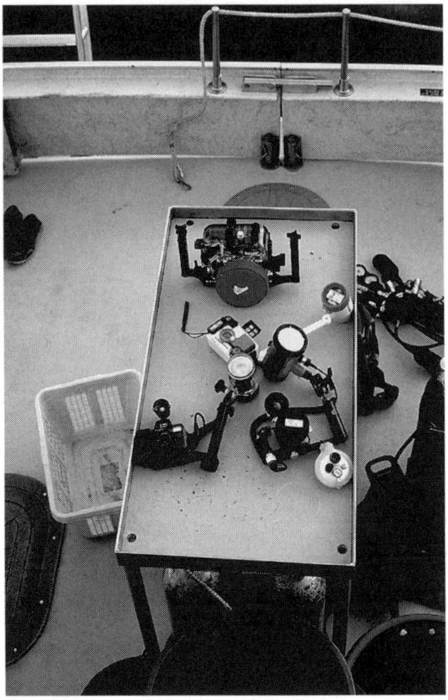

Figure 3-20 *Many dive boats have a special shelf or table set aside for camera systems.*

Get Your Camera System Its Own "Passport"

Odds are, many—if not all—of your camera system components were made in a country other than the one in which you live. Thus, when returning home from a overseas dive trip, don't be surprised if your friendly customs agents ask pointed questions regarding where and when you purchased all your shiny new photo equipment.

You can avoid customs hassles by registering your equipment ahead of time with your closest customs office. In the United States, the customs service can issue you a form called the *Certificate of Registration for Personal Effects Taken Abroad.* Think of this form as a passport for your photo gear. It proves that the applicable import duties on your equipment have long since been paid—and will help you and your equipment move through customs with less hassle.

POST-DIVE CAMERA SYSTEM MAINTENANCE AND STORAGE

If the steps involved in pre-dive camera system assembly are what you must do in order to take pictures under water, the steps involved in post-dive maintenance are what you must do in order to take pictures under water...more than once. Early in this chapter, we discussed the enemies that can begin attacking your camera system the minute you surface from the dive. This section covers how to defeat them.

Rinsing and Soaking On-board

Most dive boats have a fresh-water rinse bucket or container of some kind. More enlightened charter operations provide a separate rinse container for cameras and video systems. If you are diving from a boat, in salt water, you need to get your camera system into the best available rinse bucket as soon after you surface as possible (Figure 3-21).

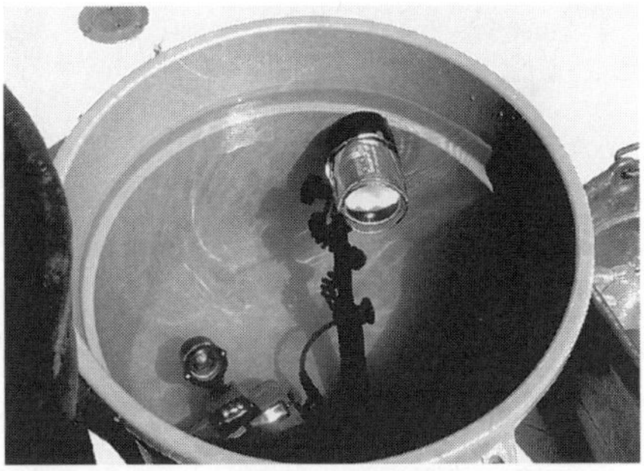

Figure 3-21 *It is best to get your camera system into the dive boat's rinse bucket as soon as you surface.*

Once your system is in the rinse bucket, let it soak for at least 30 minutes. If the rinse bucket is not reserved solely for cameras, keep an eye on it—or, sure enough, some careless diver will drop a weight belt or other heavy object on top of your camera. Even if you are fortunate enough to have access to a "cameras only" rinse bucket, remember to put your lens cap or dome port cover back in place, lest some other camera system scratch yours.

If there is no rinse tank on board, try to bring your own. A small container slightly larger than your camera system will do. Remember that you will need to bring your own fresh water if there is none on board or if its quality is questionable. These are the same steps you will need to take if diving from the beach.

These examples underscore the importance of calling ahead to research the facilities available on dive boats and at resorts. It is tough to prepare for lack of fresh water or rinse tanks on dive boats, or the possibility of brackish running water in hotel rooms, unless you learn about it beforehand.

In extreme circumstances, there may be no practical means of bringing fresh water with you. In this case, immerse your camera system in a container of *salt* water and leave it there until you can get back to where there is fresh water for rinsing and soaking. The logic here is, if you cannot rinse the salt water off your system, you can at least prevent that salt water from drying by keeping the entire system wet.

If you are done shooting pictures for the day, you can remove the tray and strobe arm from your system, if doing so will not interfere with your ability to safely transport the system back to your home or hotel. However, you should not open the battery compartment, or disconnect your sync cord, until you complete the next step.

Final Rinsing and Drying

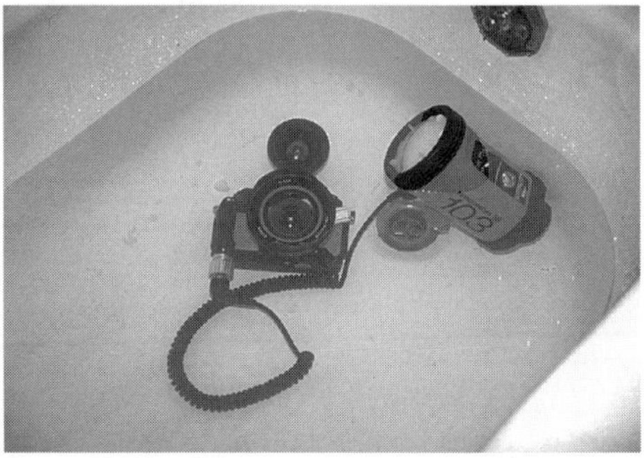

Figure 3-22 *When you return to your home or hotel room, let your camera system soak for at least an additional hour.*

As soon as you return to your home or hotel, immerse your camera system in clean, fresh water for at least an hour (Figure 3-22). This will do a more thorough job of dissolving trapped salts and minerals than the 30-minute soak in the boat's rinse tank was able to. (Remember that after having several other camera systems and miscellaneous pieces of dive equip- ment dipped in it, the water in that rinse tank was probably no longer completely "fresh.")

Giving your camera an hour-long or greater soaking after you return to your home or hotel is also a good idea if you dive in anything but the purest fresh water. Most fresh water has a fairly high level of dissolved sediments and minerals. Soaking your camera system for an hour after each day of use helps keeps these contaminants from building up in cracks and crevices.

If your pre-travel research shows that the remote resort you plan to visit has less-than-pure running water, you will have to go to the extreme of taking rinse water with you. This may not exactly be convenient. Therefore, you should probably take the quality of available rinse water into account when selecting a dive boat or resort.

After this more thorough soaking, towel your system off, then allow it to air dry completely before unloading or re-loading film.

Disassembly and Storage

If you will be using your system again within a day or two, there may be no need to completely disassemble your camera system between rolls. As long as you leave your strobe and camera batteries in place, and do not disconnect your sync cord from its strobe and camera sockets, it is probably safe to leave your system assembled between dives.

Any time that you expose an O-ring to air, however, you should perform the five steps of complete O-ring maintenance outlined early in this chapter. A good example of this would be servicing the film compartment O-ring in an amphibious camera each time you change film.

Also, it is a good idea to remove your strobe arm and camera tray from the camera or housing if the system will sit idle for more than a few hours. This will help prevent salt or minerals from building up in the spaces between these items.

If it will be more than a couple days before you use the camera again, or if you have not done so for three or four rolls of film, you should completely disassemble your system. Disconnect the sync cord, and remove the batteries from the strobe and camera.

There is a danger in storing your system for extended periods with pressure on the O-rings. This can flatten the O-rings so that they lose their ability to function. Yet, at the same time, having O-rings in place helps keep dust and moisture form entering the camera body. One solution to this problem that many photographers use is to replace the O-rings in their cameras with a used set when storing the system for extended periods.

Nikonos users can obtain special body and lens caps from several sources. These help keep the lens and camera body dust- and moisture-free, and eliminate the need to store the body with the lens attached.

Once your system is rinsed, completely dried and disassembled, store it in a dust- and moisture-proof container. This is a function that the hard-shelled camera cases described earlier perform well.

Flooding: Surviving Every Underwater Photographer's Worst Nightmare

Flooded. The word is enough to send chills down every underwater photographer's spine. It is not just your camera system at risk; if you are in the middle of a diving vacation when this tragedy strikes, flooding may leave you without any way to capture memories of the balance of your stay.

Prevention is, of course, the best way to deal with the possibility of flooding. If you follow the procedures outlined in this chapter, the chances of experiencing a flooded camera are minimal. Nevertheless, even with the most conscientious preparation and care, floodings sometimes occur.

If this misfortune should happen to you, realize that—despite prompt action—there may be nothing you can do to save your camera. On the other hand, prompt action may at least minimize the damage. Being as you have nothing to lose, it is best to act as if the situation is at least partially salvageable.

There are several ways in which a flooded underwater camera system may announce itself. A strobe may not fire, or it may attempt to fire repeatedly without being triggered. Film may not advance, or the advance mechanism may feel sluggish. You may see a steady stream of bubbles leak from an opening in the camera or housing. A lens, viewfinder or clear camera housing that is partially filled with water is an excellent indication that something is amiss.

Whatever the indication of flooding, resist the temptation to rocket to the surface with your camera. No mere collection of metal, glass and plastic is worth the pain and expense of a trip to the chamber. Still, there are several actions you should take right away.

If you are shooting a housed SLR, point the housing downward. This will cause the water to collect in the dome port or flat port extension. In so doing, you may spare your camera body, and even your lens, entirely.

Whatever system you are shooting, begin an immediate—but slow—ascent. After surfacing, swim to the boat or shore. If possible, hold your camera or housing out of the water on the way.

At this point, the precise steps you should follow will vary, depending on the type of camera system you are using. You should be prepared ahead of time by reading whatever your owner's manual may say about handling a flooded camera. Additionally, if there is a book available that dedicates itself solely to your system, buy it—especially if it has a section that lists the steps to follow in the event of an accidental flooding.

Here are some general procedures that will apply to most camera systems.

- *Avoid the temptation to immediately immerse your entire system in the boat's rinse tank*—This will not only fail to flush out the contaminated water, it may only serve to force this water further into the system.
- *Immediately remove any film and batteries from the system* (Figure 3-A)—Once exposed to water, film will de-emulsify, clogging gears and other precision mechanisms. Batteries, once exposed to water, may begin leaking corrosive acids. This is particularly true when exposed to sea water. Discard any soaked batteries and film you remove. They are of no further value.
- *After emptying all contaminated water from your system, flush the affected area with a gentle stream of fresh water*—The trick here is to rinse only that portion of the camera system that flooded. You do not want to get water into areas that remained dry.

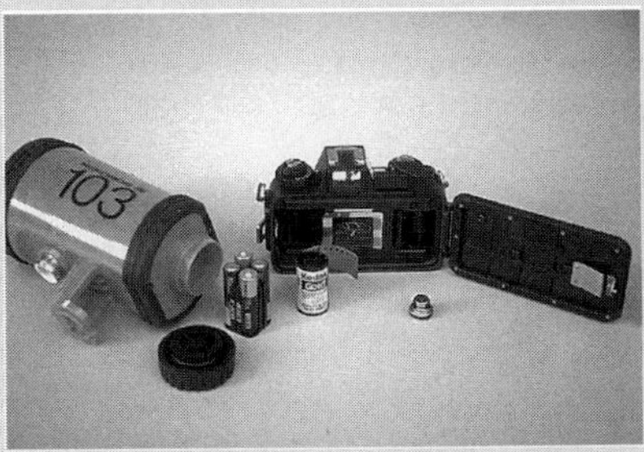

Figure 3-A *If you suspect flooding, immediately remove the film and batteries from your camera system.*

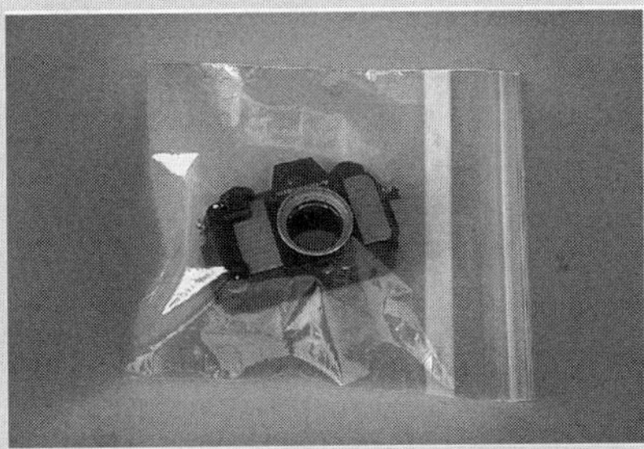

Figure 3-B *Your service center will most likely have you ship your camera system to them sealed in a plastic bag.*

- *Seal the system inside a plastic bag* (Figure 3-B)—Your goal here is to prevent any water that has entered the camera from drying and leaving behind a residue of salt, minerals, corrosives or other contaminants.

As soon as you return to your home, hotel or another suitable work area, there will be some more extensive procedures you must perform. These procedures will vary, depending on the type of camera system and the severity of the flood.

If possible, call the service center that you will be sending the camera to, tell them exactly what has happened and the steps you have taken thus far. Be prepared to write down a list of instructions they will give you. If this is not possible, consult the best available guidebook to your system for a list of steps to follow.

You may be directed to open and remove the camera's electronic circuit board. This will require use of a very small screwdriver. Another common recommendation is to soak the affected parts in de-ionized water or a mixture of fresh water and vinegar. Another common recommendation is that, once you have rinsed the affected parts as thoroughly as possible, you dry them gently with a hair dryer.

Once you have done everything your guidebook or repair center suggests, it is time to send the camera off for professional service. No matter how minor the flood, or how prompt your action, it is unlikely you can continue to use the system without causing further damage.

When shipping, seal the system inside a plastic bag, then place the bag inside a well-padded box. Use an overnight shipping service and insure your package for the camera's replacement value.

As we said earlier, prevention is the best way to handle flooding. With proper care, flooding is not something of which you need to live in constant terror. On the other hand, in the unlikely event it may occur, it helps to be prepared.

Because no amount of prompt action may be sufficient, one of the best means of being prepared is to take out a rider on your homeowner's or renter's insurance that covers the replacement value of your underwater camera equipment. This way, if your best efforts are not enough, a minor misfortune need not result in a total loss.

THE NEED FOR PROFESSIONAL SERVICE

Just as your regulator needs periodic, professional service, so does your underwater camera system. Even though you do a conscientious job of maintaining your system, before and after dives, there are still important maintenance procedures that require professional skills.

The Danger of Ignoring O-Rings You Can't See or Get To

For every camera O-ring that you can see, get to and service, there is an average of two that you cannot. If ignored, these O-rings can flatten, crack or deform, allowing water to enter the camera or housing. To ensure every O-ring and seal continues to do the job it is supposed to, your camera or housing and strobe must be thoroughly disassembled, cleaned and serviced by a trained professional. At this time, the technician will replace any O-rings that, if left unchecked, might cause problems in the future.

The Other Benefits of Professional Service

While your camera or housing and strobe is in for service, the technician can also inspect moving parts for wear, check electronic circuitry and perform other valuable tests. There is considerable value in simply having someone who has worked on hundreds of systems like yours check your system out. If there are likely to be future problems caused by worn or malfunctioning parts, a trained and experienced technician can usually find and correct these problems long before they arise.

When and Where to Get the Service You Need

Earlier, we compared the need for periodic camera system maintenance to the need for annual regulator service. It's a good analogy. Every time you get your regulator overhauled, send your camera system in for service as well.

The proper service facility for your system will depend on its make and model. Some pieces of underwater camera equipment can only be serviced at the factory. Others can be serviced by factory-authorized technicians closer to home.

It is best to have your system worked on by a technician who specializes in underwater camera systems like yours. Consult your SSI Dealer for recommendations on where to send your camera for its periodic service.

CHAPTER 3 REVIEW

1. When taking cameras under water, we ask them to face challenges that do not exist on land. Chief among these is the ____.

2. Water containing salt, electrolytes, or ionized particles is particularly destructive to sensitive electronics and ____.

3. Unless you dive in unusually pure, fresh water, your camera system's nooks, crannies, cracks and crevices will, after the dive, still contain water laced with ______________, ______________, ______________ or ______________.

4. Moist salt crystals can cause an ________________________ that seemingly dissolves aluminum casings and other metal parts. Salt build-up can ________________________ together as effectively as a weld.

5. A considerable portion of preparing your camera for use under water involves the removal, cleaning, inspection, lubrication and proper reinstallation of ________________________.

6. What you are looking for when you inspect your O-rings are ______________, ________________, ______________ or ________________________.

7. Some strobes enable you to ________________ them independently of the camera. There should be a bright flash of light, after which the strobe should fully recycle within ________________ ____.

8. The best way to protect your unassembled camera system when traveling long distances is to use a ________________________________.

9. If you are diving from a boat, in salt water, you need to get your camera system into the best available ____________________________ as soon after you surface as possible.

10. For every camera O-ring you can see, get to and service, there is ________________________ ________________________ you cannot. This is why your camera system needs professional service on a regular basis.

SHOOTING UNDER WATER

4

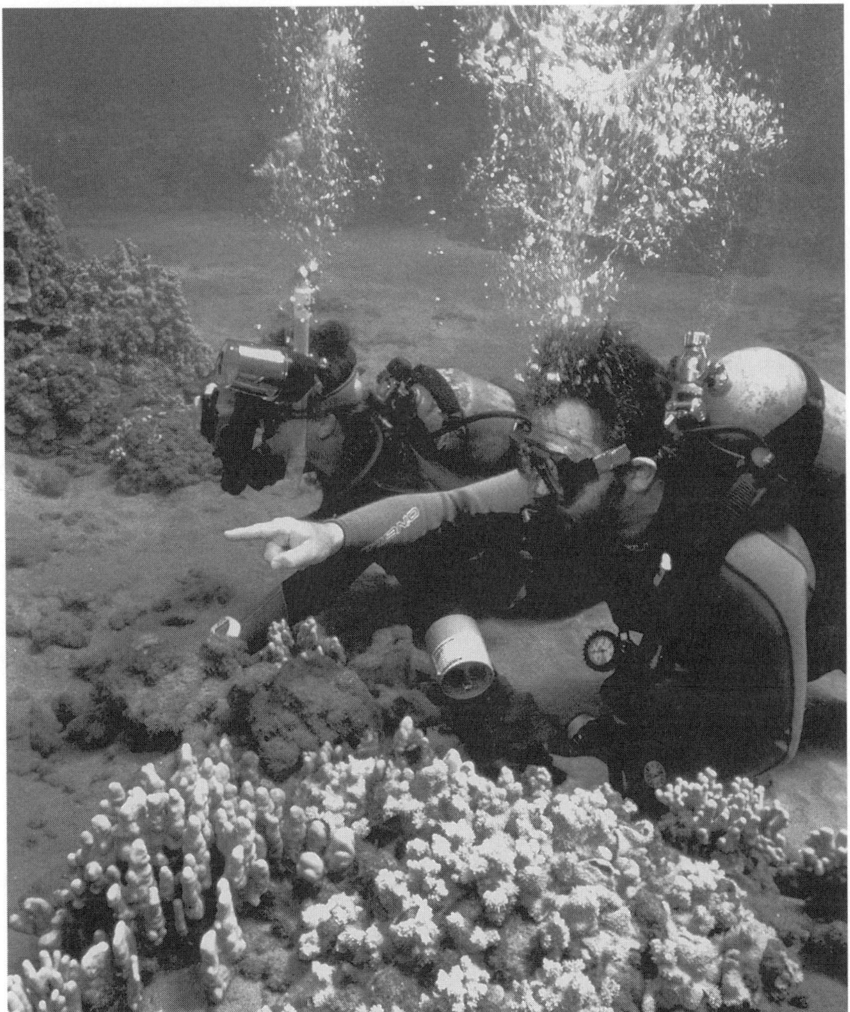

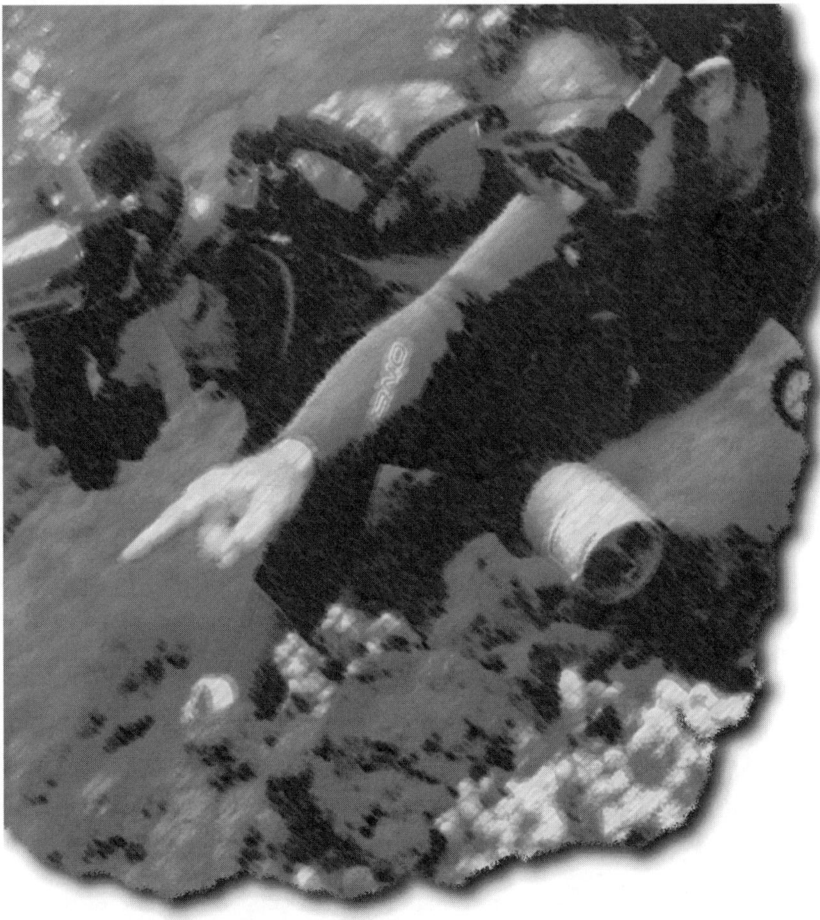

CHAPTER 4: SHOOTING UNDER WATER

You have mastered the necessary background information and properly assembled your camera system for use. Now you are ready to take your first underwater shots. That's what this chapter is all about.

We'll begin by discussing the three basic principles that are behind many of the steps in taking those shots. Then we will elaborate on each individual step in detail.

THREE BASIC PRINCIPLES OF UNDERWATER PHOTOGRAPHY

The three most basic principles of underwater photography are: *get close; get low;* and *shoot up*. There are additional factors that contribute to successful underwater image taking; however, according to most professional underwater photographers, none eclipse these three. In this section, we explain why each of these three principles are so important.

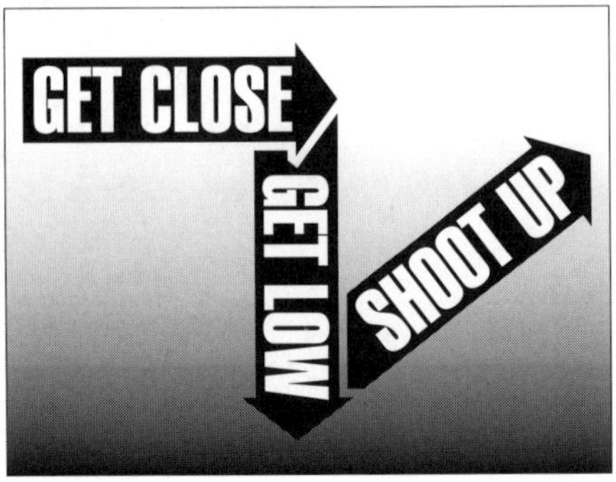

Get Close

Would you be content taking underwater pictures consisting solely of silhouettes? Or of monochromatic blue underwater landscapes? Of course not.

This is why most photographers realize the importance of strobes in underwater image taking. Without strobe lighting, underwater photos consist only of silhouettes and blue landscapes. We need strobe lighting to restore the light and color water filters out.

What many amateur underwater photographers don't realize, however, is that even the best underwater strobes have severe limitations. Among them is that virtually no strobe, no matter how big or how powerful, can *effectively* illuminate subjects much farther than four feet (one-and-a-quarter metres) from the camera.

Technically, you can detect the presence of strobe light, in some photos, as far away as eight feet (two-and-a-half metres) from the camera. However, as Figure 4-1 shows, there is a sharp drop off in the quantity of this light at about half this distance. This means, if you attempt taking an underwater photo of a subject any farther away than this, the resulting picture will appear as though you weren't using a strobe at all! In other words, it won't be worth taking.

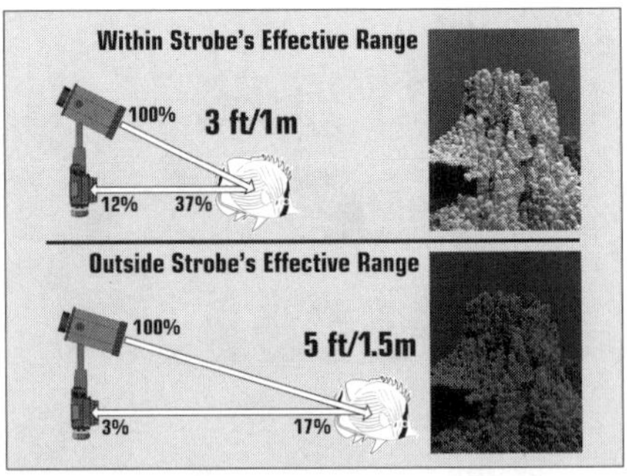

Figure 4-1 *Once subject matter is more than 4 feet (1.25 metres) from the camera, there is usually insufficient strobe light returning from the subject to create an adequate exposure.*

The majority of photos taken by professional underwater photographers are shot from a distance of three to four feet (one to one-and-a-quarter metres). An additional benefit of shooting up close includes the fact that there will be a reduced quantity of suspended particles between your lens and your subject. This leads to sharper photos and reduced backscatter.

Get Low

We generally look down when we swim over the bottom. The fish, coral and other formations we see fascinate us. Therefore, when first shooting pictures under water, it's only natural to shoot them in the same direction we look: *down.*

However, when we get those pictures back, the subject matter often appears less interesting than the way we remember it. The once-vibrant bottom is now a disjointed collection of browns and blues that run together. The pictures are nowhere near as exciting to look at as the ones we see in dive magazines. Why is that?

The answer lies in how our eyes and mind process the information we see when we look down. Our eyes are more sensitive to light than film, so they see the bottom differently. More significantly, our brains process the information they receive from our eyes in a highly sophisticated manner—one that separates moving objects, such as fish, from static objects, such as coral.

When we freeze the objects we see by taking their picture, our brains can no longer separate foreground objects from background objects. The results are seldom as interesting as they appeared to the naked eye.

For this reason, wise underwater photographers separate their primary subject from similar background objects by shooting that subject from its side or from slightly below. In the resulting pictures, the primary subject stands out distinctly in front of a blue water background—such as you see in Figure 4-2.

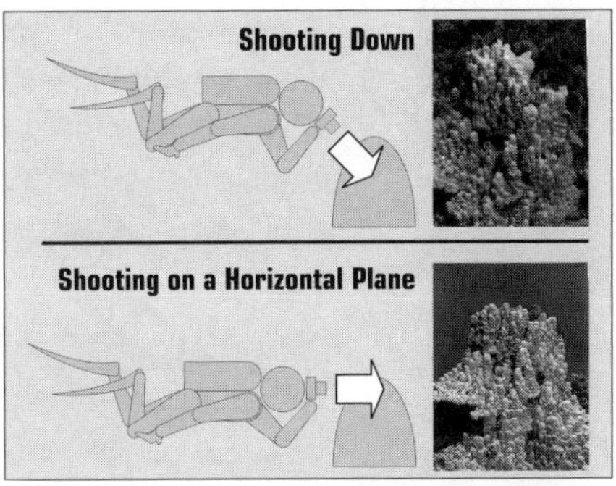

Figure 4-2 *When you shoot looking down, the scenery tends to run together, resulting in cluttered, uninteresting photos. When shot from the side, your subject matter is separated from that below it by a blue water background. This generally results in more pleasing photographs.*

As a general rule, never take a shot if your camera points any farther down than a horizontal plane. As we'll discuss next, your best pictures often result from aiming your camera upward at an acute angle.

Shoot Up

Look at the photos that fill the pages of any major diving magazine. What you'll see is that most of the photos are taken at what photo pros call an *acute angle*. This means that the camera is pointing upward at a 45 degree angle—or higher (Figure 4-3). The potential benefits of shooting this way include:

- **Texture:** You can often capture the texture of the surface, including the reflection of the sky on its multi-faceted wave faces. This helps convey both depth and water clarity, and adds to the drama of the photograph.
- **Background Color:** You create a blue background for your primary subjects which changes from a light blue at the top to a darker blue at the bottom. This further conveys the sense of depth (Figure 4-4).

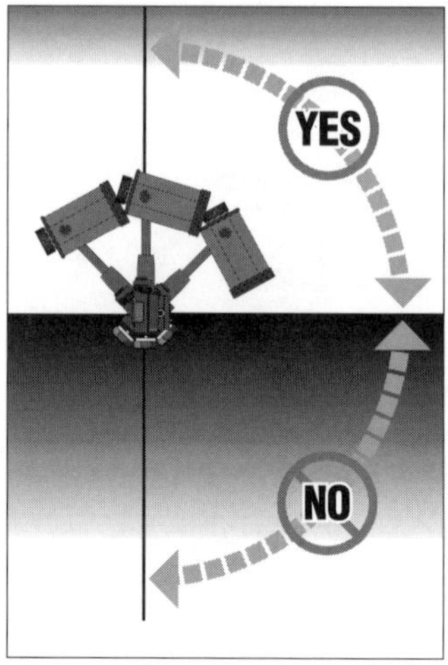

Figure 4-3 *Avoid shots in which your camera points any further down than a horizontal plane. The best pictures generally result from pointing the camera upward at a 45 degree angle.*

To shoot this way, you'll need to be well below your subject. Hovering vertical next to walls or wrecks makes this possible, as does taking advantage of sand channels adjacent to good photographic subject matter.

If you watch professional underwater photographers at work, you'll notice that they often locate an environmentally safe patch of sand or rock adjacent to their subject, then settle on this spot—not with their feet or knees, but with their shoulder, or the fingertips of one hand. This enables them to shoot upward at the maximum possible angle, for the most dramatic results.

To learn more about skills that may enable you to shoot nearly any underwater subject at an acute angle, the accompanying article *This Model Is Not a Trained Professional...*, on page 82.

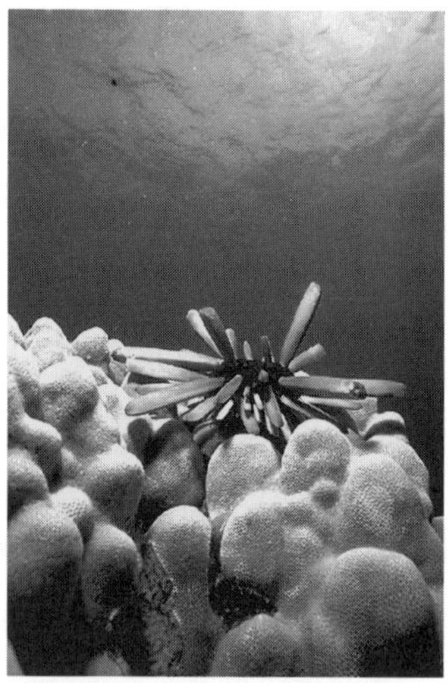

Figure 4-4 *By shooting at an upward angle, you can often capture the texture of the surface and the change in color that indicates deeper water.*

TAKING YOUR FIRST UNDERWATER SHOTS

The section that follows is really what this book is all about: Taking your first successful underwater photographs. If you are enrolled in an *Underwater Photography* Specialty Course, or doing a guided photo dive, odds are your Instructor will be there helping you with each of the following steps. While you can fumble through these steps on your own, having the guidance of a trained professional is really the best way to learn.

Get the Edge Before You Leave Home

Each year, thousands of divers buy brand-new underwater camera systems. Many of these divers wait until they leave for a vacation to use these systems. *Bad idea.*

These divers either labor under the misconception that taking good underwater photos requires little practice or preparation, or they think that there is nothing of value they can do with their camera systems unless they are in warm, clear tropical water. Both assumptions are wrong.

Here are the facts:

- *Yes, taking good underwater photos can be surprisingly easy. It is not, however, a mindless pursuit—nor can it be easily learned through trial and error. You need both preparation and practice.*
- *You need not be in warm, tropical water to spend worthwhile time with your camera system. In fact, you'll be surprised how much you can accomplish in your local SSI Dealer's pool.*

Early in this book, we recommended taking an *Underwater Photography* Specialty Course from your local SSI Dealer. This course will likely entail one or more pool or confined water sessions. If you cannot do this, see if you can arrange a pool session with one of your SSI Dealer's photo experts. Either way, you'll be surprised at how much you can accomplish.

During your pool or confined water sessions:

- *Your Instructor may have you work on the buoyancy control and camera handling exercises outlined on pages 83 and 84, or similar exercises. These will greatly enhance your control of your camera system and your comfort in the water. Even more important, they will help ensure that the environment does not pay for your decision to become an underwater photographer.*
- *He or she may also have you take a number of practice shots in the pool. These will help you gain experience handling the camera, shooting from the proper distance, framing your subjects and composing interesting shots.*

Many of the most experienced photo pros make regular trips to the pool. It enables them to test shoot new camera and strobe combinations, calibrate lens coverage and focus, and develop exposure tables for different strobes and film speeds.

You'll find the time you spend in the pool enjoyable and rewarding. More importantly, you will discover that when you get to the open water, you are much better prepared to make every minute count.

Entering the Water with Camera Equipment

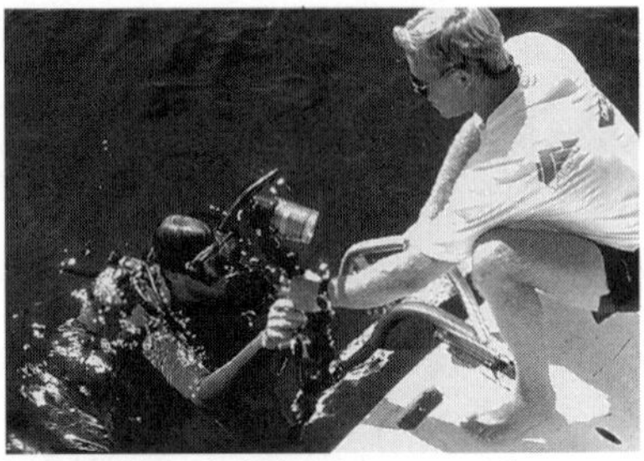

Figure 4-5 *It is best to enter the water first, then have a buddy or crew-person hand you your camera system.*

What is the best way to enter the water with camera equipment? Not to do it. At least not from a boat. Jumping into the water with your camera system in hand puts unnecessary strain on it—not to mention the fact it increases the chances of your dropping and losing it.

The better way to get your camera system into the water is to enter without the camera system, then have a crewperson hand it down to you. When you get ready to exit the water, reverse this procedure (Figure 4-5).

Determining the Right Camera Settings and Strobe Angle

As soon as you are under water, it's time to do a number of things. First, you should examine your system for any signs of leakage. This may include a steady stream of bubbles coming from anywhere on the system, or water visible inside the lens or viewfinder. While you are examining the lens, displace any air bubbles that may be sticking to the outside of the lens by making a sweeping motion of your hand in front of it. If your lens has an external diopter attached to it, remove this auxiliary lens and displace any air bubbles that may remain between it and the primary lens.

Now it is time to double check your camera settings and strobe angle. If you are shooting a housed disposable camera, determining your camera settings is easy—there aren't any! If you are shooting an amphibious camera or housed SLR, the procedures are slightly more complex. If you are taking the SSI *Underwater Photography* Specialty Course, your Instructor will help you with these settings.

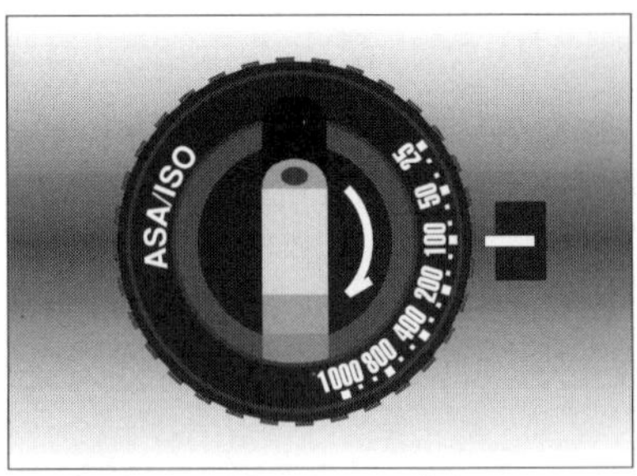

Figure 4-6 *ISO selector dial.*

- **ISO:** The first thing to set is the ISO. This ensures that your camera's metering system is calibrated to the right film speed. Most newer SLRs, the Nikonos RS and the latest cameras from Sea & Sea, have circuits that read the DX coding right off the film canister and set the ISO automatically. If you are using a Nikonos V, you'll need to double-check or re-set the ISO selector dial on the upper left hand of the camera (Figure 4-6).

- **Shutter Speed:** As a beginner, you'll most likely be shooting in TTL mode. With a modern SLR, this means setting the camera to its *automatic* mode, or one of its *program* modes. Sea & Sea cameras are always in TTL mode, so no shutter speed adjustment is necessary. Nikonos V users should set the shutter speed selector dial to *A*, for *Aperture Priority* (Figure 4-7).

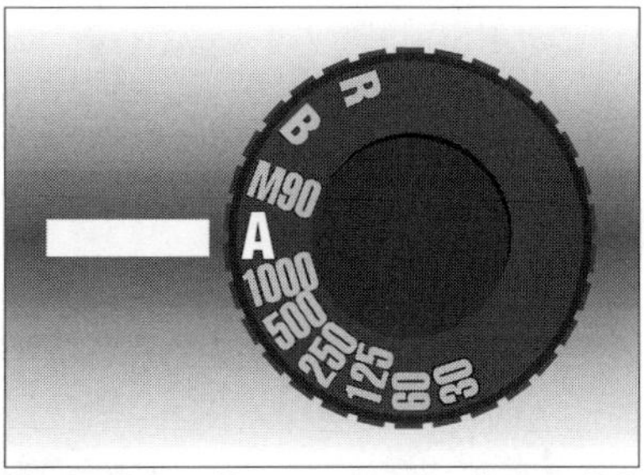

Figure 4-7 *Shutter speed selector dial.*

- **F-Stop:** This will depend primarily on your distance from your subject and on the strobe you will be using. You can usually determine the best set of *f*-stops for various distances by consulting the exposure table that comes with your strobe (Figure 4-8).

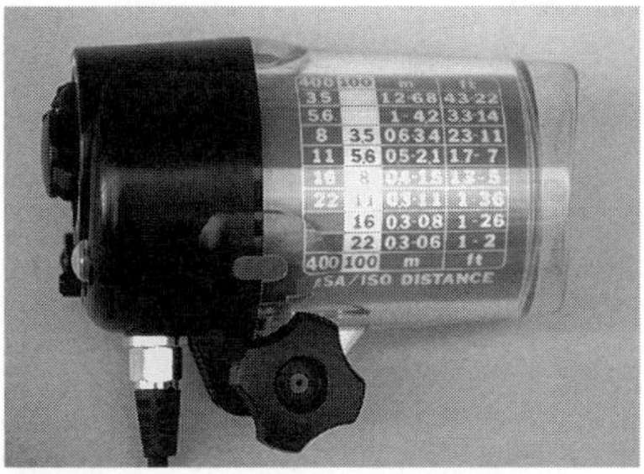

Figure 4-8 *Strobe exposure table.*

The farther away your subject matter is, the less strobe light will reach it, then return to the camera. This means that subjects that are farther away require wider apertures (lower *f*-stops). Lower *f*-stops, as you'll recall from Chapter 1, mean less depth of field. Closer subject matter can be shot at higher *f*-stops, yielding greater depth of field. This is yet another advantage of getting close to your subject.

Most Instructors have their students begin by shooting exclusively at a distance of three feet (one metre). At this distance, using ISO 100 film, most strobes require an *f*-stop of eight (*f*8) for adequate exposures. If you are using a 35mm lens, an added benefit of staying close enough to your subject to use an *f*-stop setting of eight is that it yields significantly greater depth of field than lower *f*-stops.

If you are shooting a wider-angle lens, where depth of field is not so much an issue, many experts recommend using an *f*-stop of 5.6. This *f*-stop provides an ideal exposure for a wide variety of open-water lighting conditions. By leaving your camera at this *f*-stop, you will be instantly ready to shoot nearly any photographic opportunity that presents itself—no matter how fleeting.

Each time you take a shot, you will want confirmation that you did so using an adequate exposure setting. If you choose an *f*-stop that is too high, TTL strobes will generally warn you—usually with a ready light that blinks repeatedly after you take the shot. Get in the habit of checking your ready light immediately after you depress the shutter release. If it blinks, you may need to open your aperture one *f*-stop. More than likely, however, you just need to get *closer to your subject.*

- **Distance to Subject (Focus):** If you are shooting an amphibious camera, you will need to set the lens for the proper distance to your subject. If you were shooting on land, you'd most likely be shooting subjects whose distance to the lens varied, and have to readjust the focus for each one. As a beginning underwater photographer, however, it is better to set the camera to one distance, then position yourself exactly that far from everything you shoot.

  As we mentioned earlier, most Underwater Photography Instruc-tors have students shoot at a distance of three feet (one metre) (Figure 4-9). You probably remember from your beginning scuba course, however, that objects that *appear* to be this far away, are actually four feet (one-and-a-quarter metres) away. No problem. If it appears to be this close to your eyes, it will also appear to be that close to the camera's lens.

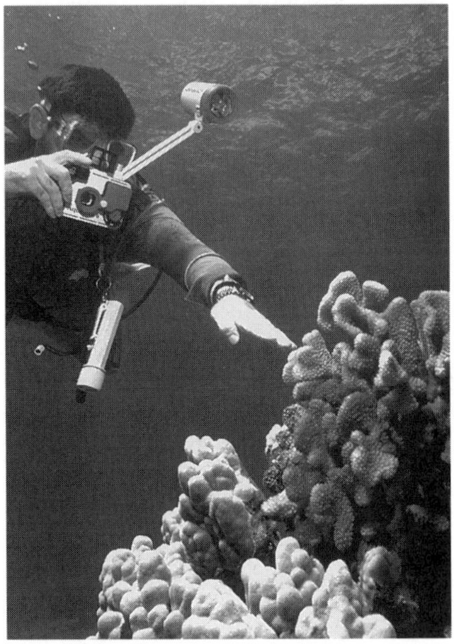

Figure 4-9 *Most Instructors recommend that students begin shooting at a distance of 3 feet (1 metre). This puts subject matter just out of arm's reach.*

- **Strobe Angle:** Earlier in this chapter, we covered the three basic rules governing all underwater photography. There is a single basic rule for strobe photography. *Never illuminate the water between your lens and your subject.*

  Unless you are fortunate enough to shoot in extremely clear water, there will almost always be suspended particles between you and your subject. These may be largely invisible to the camera—unless the light from the strobe hits them and bounces back into the camera lens (Figure 4-10). This is what we referred to earlier in the book as *backscatter*.

To avoid this, you want to aim your strobe so that the leading edge of the strobe's beam just touches the front edge of your subject (Figure 4-11). Additionally, because light from a strobe positioned this way hits suspended particles at an angle, this light is less likely to reflect back into the camera's lens.

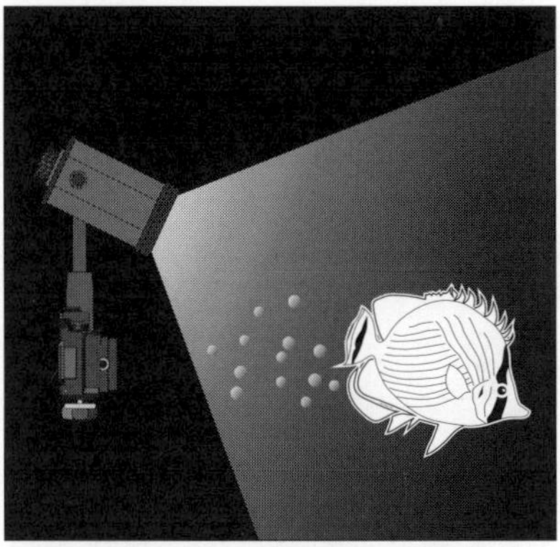

Figure 4-10 *When light from your strobe hits suspended particles, then bounces back into your camera's lens, it may produce backscatter...*

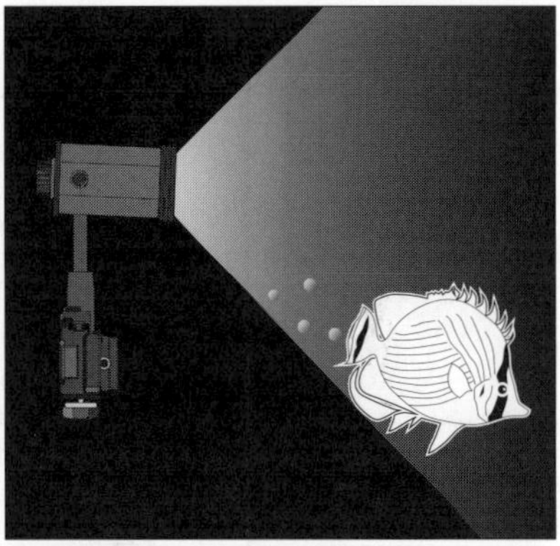

Figure 4-11 *...Aiming your strobe so that the leading edge of its beam just touches the front of your subject can help reduce backscatter.*

Theoretically, you could position your strobe on either side of your camera, or even below it, and still hit the subject from an angle that minimized the problem of backscatter. The most natural-looking angle for strobe light, however, is to position it above and slightly off to one side of the camera, so that it mimics the angle of the sun.

As a beginner, you will most likely shoot with the strobe and its arm attached to your camera tray. A good way to aim a strobe that is set up this way is to hold the camera at arm's length, with the lens pointed toward you. Now look up and point the strobe so that it is aimed at a spot slightly above and behind you (Figure 4-12).

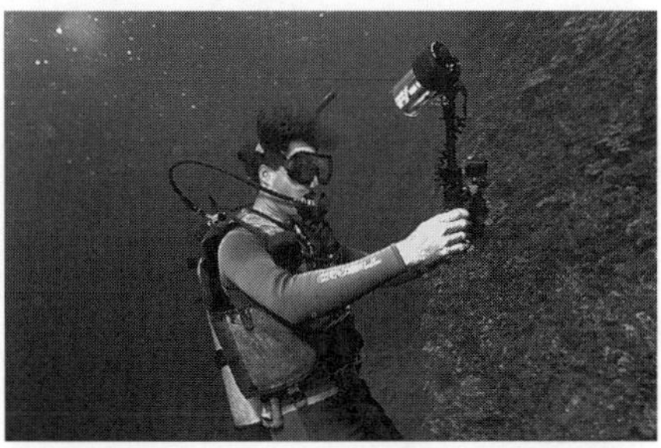

Figure 4-12 *A good way to determine where your strobe is aimed is to point the camera towards you while holding it at arm's length.*

As you gain experience, you may choose to do as many professional underwater photographers do: hand hold your strobe. If so, you'll probably want to take advantage of an aiming light (Figure 4-13), such as we described in Chapter 1.

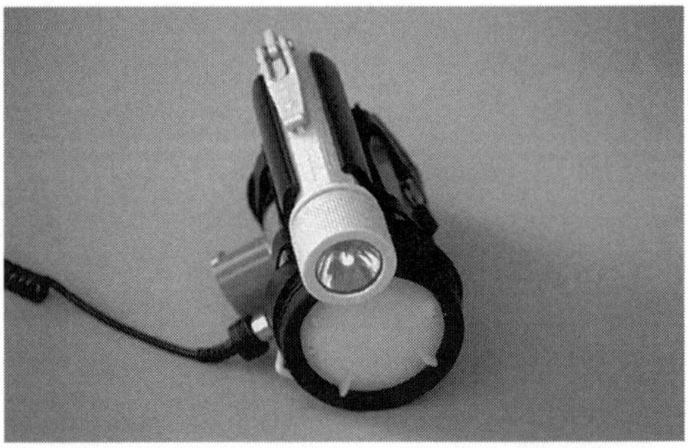

Figure 4-13 *If you choose to hand hold your strobe, you will probably want to take advantage of an aiming light.*

This Model Is *Not* a Trained Professional: *Do* Try This at Home

Many new underwater photographers report that not once during their beginning scuba class did they ever feel as awkward and as uncoordinated as they do using a camera under water for the first time. Without prior practice or preparation, handling an underwater camera can be a frustrating experience. You may feel off balance and out of control. Holding the camera steady enough to take a decent shot may seem next to impossible.

If getting decent shots were the only problem, it would be bad enough. There is, however, a second problem that makes things much worse.

Divers who are off balance and out of control are in no position to protect the environment. They stand on, sit on or crash into coral, destroying formations that took dozens of years to develop. They uproot aquatic plants and disturb delicate habitats. No wonder so many resort operators put new underwater photographers on a par with insensitive game and artifact hunters.

The first time you enter the aquatic environment with an underwater camera system, you want to make every minute count. You want total control of your camera system so that composing good underwater shots is easy. Additionally, you want everyone who sees you to think of you as an environmentally sensitive diver—not as a bull in a china shop.

Great. Now how do you make this happen?

Begin by making an honest assessment of your present diving skills. To successfully control your camera system under water, your mastery of basic skills such as buoyancy control, body position and propulsion must be excellent. To see how your present skills rate, try these exercises in your dive store's pool or at your local dive site:

- *Hovering*—You should be able to hover motionless, in shallow water, in both vertical and horizontal positions. You will need to be able to hover vertically to take pictures along the sides of steep walls, drop-

Identifying Good Subject Matter

At this point, you are in the water, your camera is ready to go—all you need now is something to take a picture of. Your best choices will depend, in part, on whether you are in fresh or salt water, warm or cold water, and on what the local environment can provide.

As a beginner, you will likely be shooting a lens with a focal length of 28mm to 35mm. This means that, at a distance of no more than three to four feet (90cm to 1.2m), your subject matter can occupy an area no larger than two feet by three feet (60cm by 90cm). This is roughly the size of your buddy's head and shoulders. It is a considerably smaller area than you can see with your eyes at the same distance.

offs and tall wrecks. The ability to hover horizontally will enable you to work over fragile aquatic life without hurting it. A good test of your ability to hover in a horizontal position is to tuck your chin to your chest. If your body is truly horizontal, you will be able to see everything going on behind you (Figure 4-A).

- *The Helicopter Turn*—This exercise tests your ability to combine buoyancy control with precision propulsion techniques. While maintaining the horizontal hover position just described, pivot 360 degree using just your fin tips (Figure 4-B).
- *The Human Tripod*—Occasionally, there will be a sandy area, adjacent to good photographic subject matter. When there is, you should be able to rest there, in a kneeling position (Figure 4-C), without stirring up sand or silt—or losing your balance and crashing into nearby coral or other delicate aquatic life.

continued on page 84...

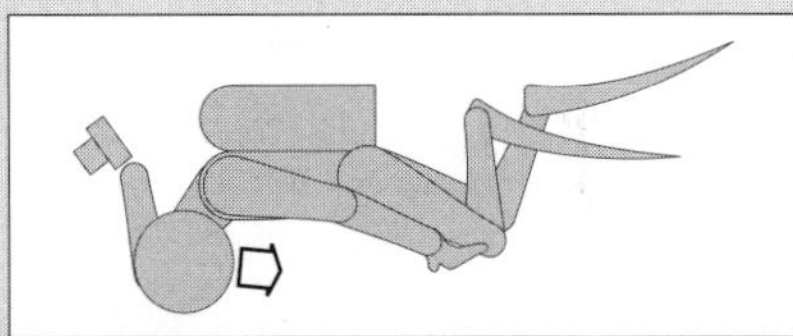

Figure 4-A *A good test of body position is to tuck your head to your chest; if your body is in proper trim, you should be able to see everything going on behind you.*

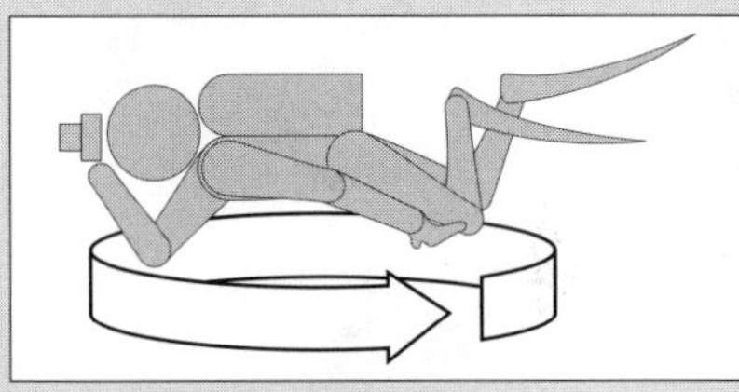

Figure 4-B *Helicopter turn.*

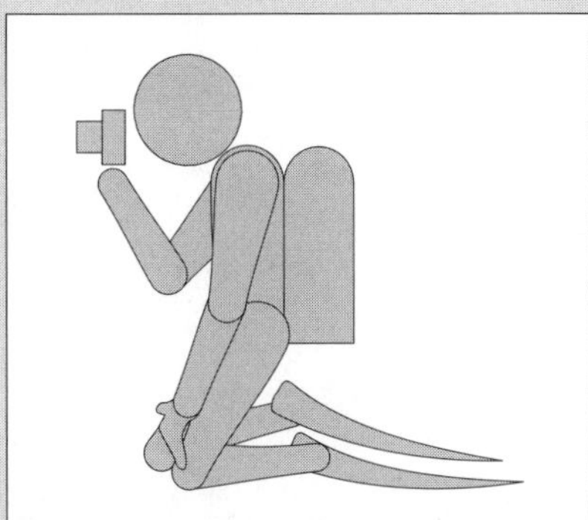

Figure 4-C *The human tripod.*

...continued from page 83

To practice this skill, pick a spot on the bottom next to a pool wall, boulder or other large object. From a hover, see if you can gently settle on this spot, in a kneeling position, with an absolute minimum of movement. Once comfortably in this position, see if you can lift off, causing minimal disturbance.

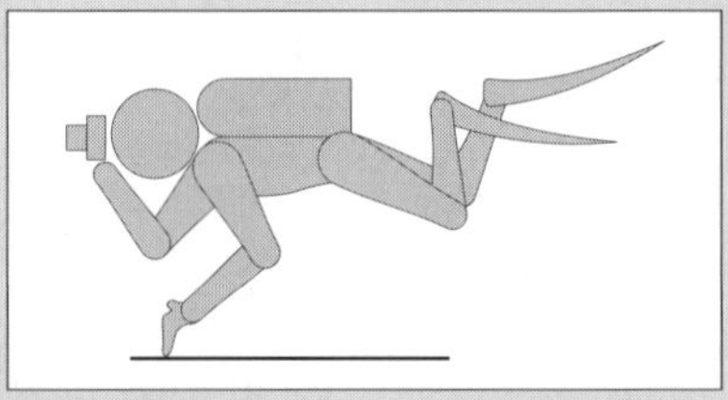

Figure 4-D *The one-finger push-up.*

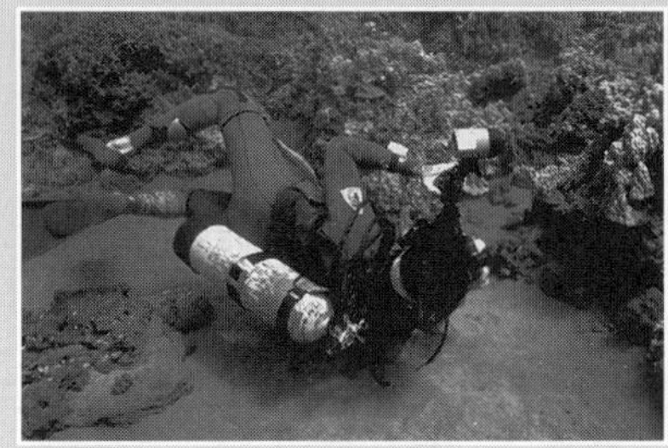

Figure 4-E *The shoulder-rest position.*

Once you master these three exercises, it is time to simulate the task of holding and carrying your underwater camera system. To avoid damage to the system itself, substitute a brick. Repeat each of the exercises described earlier while holding the brick much as you would a camera.

Also try two additional exercises:

- *The One-Finger Push-up*—While in a horizontal hover, hold the brick in front of you while balancing on a single finger of the other hand (Figure 4-D). In this position, see how close you can lower yourself toward the bottom without actually touching.
- *Shoulder Rest*—While hovering in a horizontal position, turn on your side. Now see if you can come to rest with just your shoulder touching the bottom (Figure 4-E). From this position, see if you can use your brick to take a "shot" at an upward angle.

What you may discover while mastering these exercises is that long before you make contact with the bottom, your alternate-air-source second stage, instrument console or low-pressure inflator hose do. If this occurs, it is a sign that you either need to fasten these items to your other equipment, using suitable retainers, or reposition those retainers so the offending equipment is tucked in even closer to your body.

Once you have mastered each of the exercises outlined here, you are ready to take your camera system into the open water. When you get there, you'll find you're much more confident, comfortable and in control than you would have been without this preparation and practice.

If the exercises described seem so far beyond your ability as to be impossible, consider enrolling in a buoyancy control workshop or clinic. You will be surprised at how rapidly you can make progress under the training of a skilled SSI Instructor.

Your first underwater outing with a camera should be relaxing and enjoyable. With proper preparation, it can be. Without it, you will most likely not get your money's worth from your camera system—and, worse, you may cause irreparable damage to the environment.

It is important you understand this limitation. If you do not, you will have a tendency—as you look through the viewfinder—to pull back from your subject matter in an attempt to recapture more of what you can see with your eyes. In so doing, you will pull back out of strobe range and out of your lens' pre-set zone of focus. The result will be fuzzy, blue pictures.

One way to prevent this is to imagine there is a two foot by three foot (60cm by 90cm) picture frame floating in the water in front of you, just out of arm's reach. To qualify as good subject matter, an object must be able to fit within this frame.

Here are several examples of good subject matter for beginning photographers, in a variety of environments.

- **Fresh Water:** What fresh water lacks in marine life, it often makes up for in artifacts (Figure 4-14). Good subject matter here generally consists of a head-and-shoulders picture of your buddy, who positions himself or herself behind and slightly above an interesting piece of wreckage, debris or other object (Figure 4-15). Your buddy's eyes should be no more than 18 inches (45 centimetres) from this object, and be pointed in its direction.

  A variation on this shoot is have your buddy cup his or her hands in front of them, and hold a small but interesting piece of wreckage or debris. Pictures such as these tell stories. *Once there was an everyday item whose makers never dreamed it would end up resting far below the surface of the water. Now it does—and the only people who can see it are divers.*

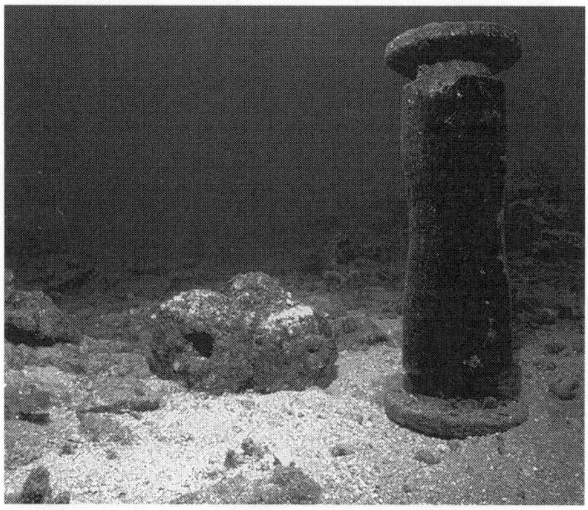

Figure 4-14 *What fresh water lacks in aquatic life, it often makes up for in artifacts.*

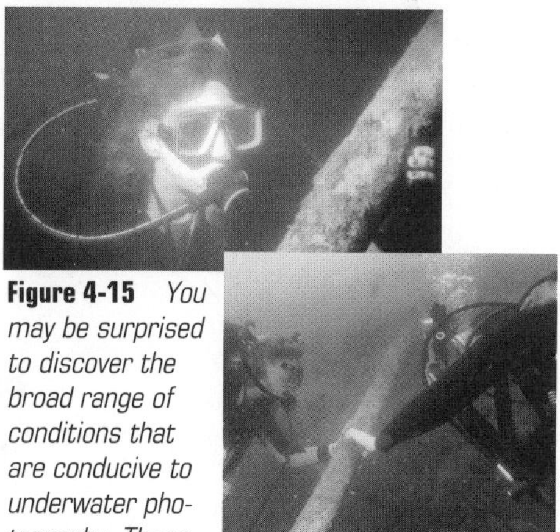

Figure 4-15 *You may be surprised to discover the broad range of conditions that are conducive to underwater photography. These photos were taken in a rock quarry with less than 6 feet (2 metres) of visibility and considerable suspended particle matter.*

Some freshwater springs offer unusually clear water. The chief attraction at these sites is the unique geology. The best shots in such an environment show divers framed by interesting rock formations.

- **Colder Ocean Water:** Large, aquatic plants, such as kelp, thrive in colder ocean water. Additionally, the rocky bottom of these environments is generally carpeted with a rich assortment of hard and soft coral-like creatures, sponges and anemones.

  A good shot here is to get close to the bottom and shoot up at your buddy, as he or she peers over a small boulder or rock formation. Your buddy should look at the aquatic life covering this formation. In environments with kelp, you can often frame the kelp stalk towering overhead as well.

- **Warm Ocean Water:** A quick look through any of the popular dive magazines will tell you that warm ocean water offers one of the richest and most diverse collections of subject matter for underwater photography. Keep in mind, however, that most of the pictures in that magazine were taken using much wider lenses than you will likely use as a beginner. Therefore, you will probably be better off choosing somewhat different subjects.

  Among the most tempting warm-water photographic subjects are colorful, tropical fish. Keep in mind, though, that it is unlikely one or two individual fish will hold still long enough for you to compose and shoot a good picture of them. Even large tropical fish will not come close enough to the camera to adequately fill your frame.

  It gets worse if you attempt to chase fish in an effort to get their picture. What you usually end up with is a largely empty frame with a speck in the middle. That speck is the south end of a north-bound fish (Figure 4-16).

  You will do much better with stationary subjects such as coral formations, sea fans and large sponges. You can shoot these subjects by themselves, or position your buddy slightly above and behind them.

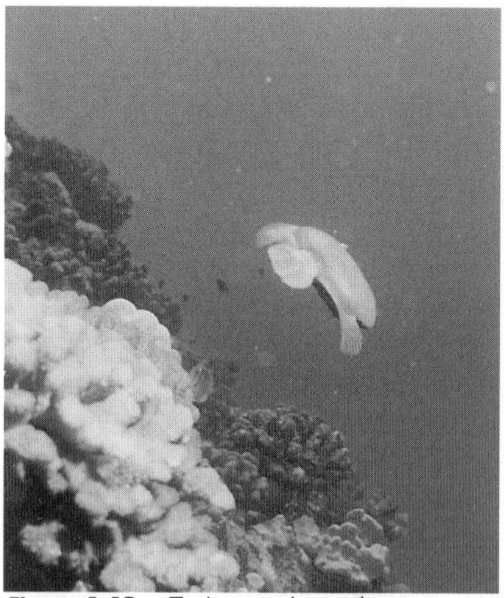

Figure 4-16 *Trying to chase down individual fish to get them on film usually results in pictures of the south end of north-bound fish.*

Notice in each of these shots that the photographer followed the basic principles of underwater photography by not only getting close to the subject, but close to the bottom as well. The results are pictures in which the bottom is framed by a solid, blue background—rather than by a jumble of other bottom formations.

Basic Composition

Having identified good subject matter, you are now closer to framing and taking the shot. As you gain more experience, you'll learn about advanced principles of composition. You'll gain an understanding of terms such as the *rule of thirds* and *shooting along diagonals*.

For right now, however, you are better off sticking with just a few basic rules of composition. They are:

- **Limit Your Subject Matter:** In each of the sample photos shown thus far, you've seen either just a primary subject (an artifact, rock or coral formation), or this primary subject in juxtaposition with a secondary subject (another diver). This simplicity helps make picture taking easy—and still leads to interesting and visually appealing pictures (Figure 4-17).

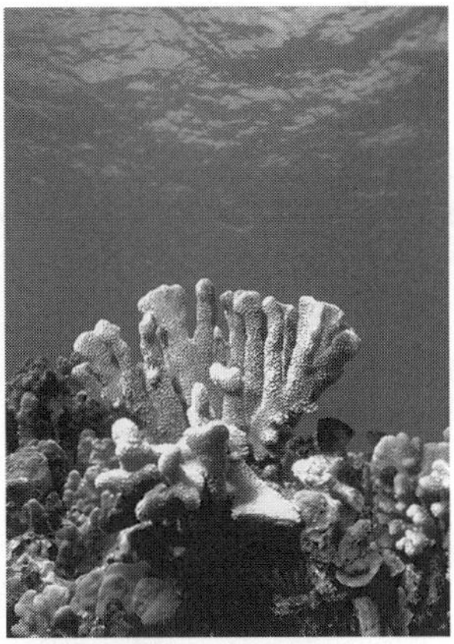

Figure 4-17 *A single, stationary object provides the best subject for your first photographs.*

- **Center Your Subject; Fill Your Frame:** Another thing you will notice about these photos is that the subject matter is centered within the picture and fills roughly two thirds of the frame. While this does not represent the most advanced photographic composition technique, it is a safe, successful technique for beginners—and a technique you will find in many award-winning photos as well (Figure 4-18).

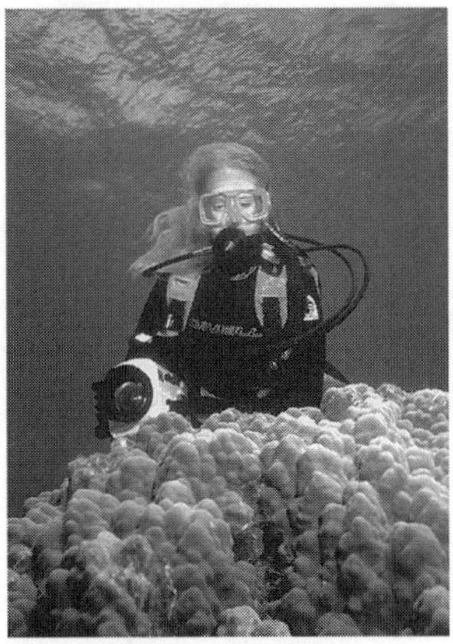

Figure 4-18 *Your first attempts at composition should involve centering your subjects and having them fill at least two-thirds of your frame.*

Many underwater photographers—beginners and experienced alike—have difficulty framing subjects using the internal rangefinder on amphibious cameras. They find they end up with pictures in which subject matter is off center, models are partially decapitated and portions of their primary subject are cut off.

If this is a problem for you, try using an external viewfinder such as we discussed in Chapter 1. Its larger eyepiece and parallax-adjustment capabilities usually solve the problem.

- **Shoot in Portrait Mode:** The design of both land and underwater cameras facilitates shooting in *landscape* (horizontal) mode. However, if you'll look, most of the underwater photos appearing in this book—as well as in any other book or magazine on diving—you'll discover the most successful underwater photos are shot in *portrait* (vertical) mode.

  Taking the majority of your underwater shots this way offers several benefits. As most of the subject matter you'll shoot is taller than wider, it better fills the frame if you shoot in portrait mode. Shooting in portrait mode lets you get more of the surface of the water, and its unique texture, in the shot. Portrait mode also gives you background that shows a more noticeable shift from light blue to dark blue (Figure 4-19).

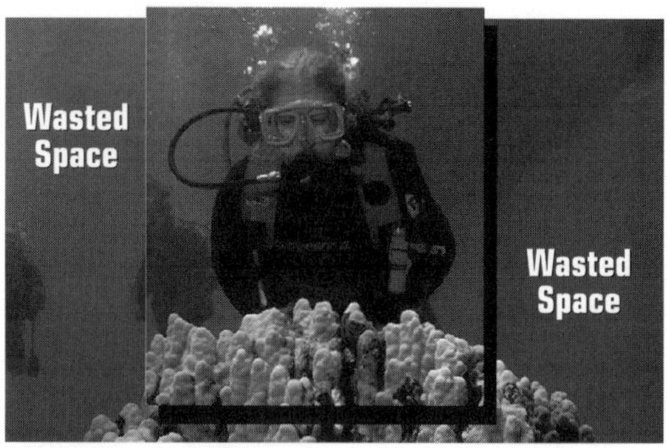

Figure 4-19 *Most subjects work best if shot in portrait mode. This enables you to get closer to your subject, fill your frame more completely and results in less wasted space.*

  Earlier in this chapter we recommended that as you search for subject matter, you imagine a picture frame floating just out of arm's reach. It also helps to imagine that picture frame two ways: in both horizontal and vertical positions. What you will discover is, more often than not, it is the vertical (portrait) position that best frames your subject matter.

  If you are in doubt as to which orientation to use for a particular subject, shoot it both ways. You can decide after the pictures are developed which way worked best.

The Importance of Consistency

At this point, you are ready to take your first picture. Having set the camera up properly, identified good subject matter and composed how that picture will fill your frame, all that remains to do is push the shutter release. Is this all there is to it? Not quite. There are three recommendations most photo pros have that are particularly applicable to beginning photographers.

- **Master One Way of Shooting First:** Ansel Adams is among the most revered photographers of all time. Yet much of his success is due to the fact that, rather than experiment with a variety of films, cameras and subject matter, he chose to master one film, one camera and one particular type of subject. Today, his portfolio of black-and-white, large-format landscapes of the American west are worth millions.

  The lesson of Ansel Adams' success is one that expert photographers share with students of all types of photography. It is: *Stick with one film, one camera system, one basic set of camera settings and one basic type of subject matter until you feel you have totally mastered them* (Figure 4-20). Only then should you expand your range—and, only then will you find doing so easy. Talk to the world's best underwater photographers; you'll find they generally agree.

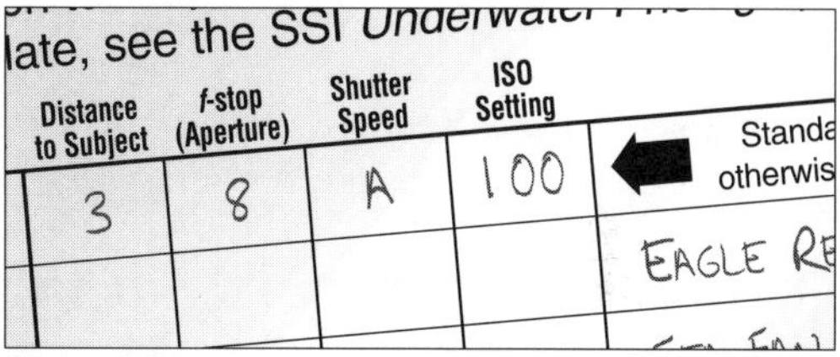

Figure 4-20 *Most experts recommend you stick with one film, one basic group of camera settings and one type of subject matter until you master them.*

- **Take More Than One Shot of the Same Subject:** The direct cost of exposing one frame of film is usually a fraction of what it costs for the opportunity to take that shot. Given this lopsided relationship, do you really want to gamble that the only picture you take of a particular subject will come out the way you want it?

  Most experienced photographers take multiple shots of the same subject (Figure 4-21). This way, if they lose

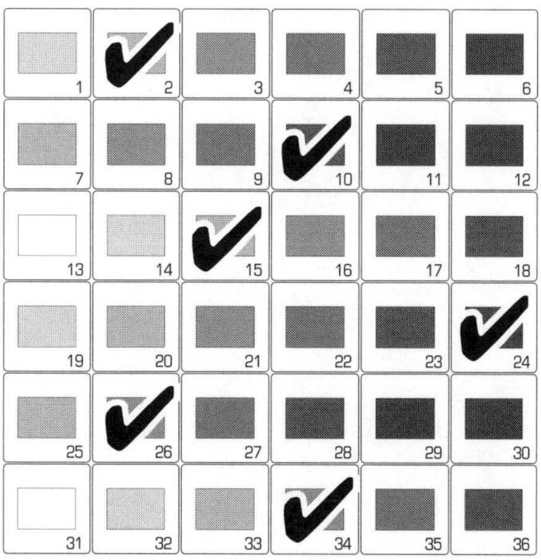

Figure 4-21 *Shoot six subjects six different ways and you are likely to end up with at least one good shot of each.*

their balance just as they depress the shutter release, if their model is momentarily distracted, or if a rogue fish decides to swim right in front of the lens, unnoticed, it will not ruin their only opportunity to capture the image. If anything, this advice is more applicable to beginners than it is to diving's more experienced photo pros.

Experienced photographers will also shoot a single subject a multitude of ways. They may experiment with portrait and landscape orientation. They may shoot the same subject from different angles. They may also *bracket* their exposures—a technique we discuss in Chapter 5.

The logic behind this is sound. The world's best photographers typically deem less than six exposures from each roll to be worth keeping. Which would you rather do—shoot 36 different subjects with no control over which six subjects turned out? Or, shoot six different subjects six different ways, so that at least one shot of each subject was likely to be worth keeping?

- **Expose as Much Film as You Can:** This is an extension of the principle that the direct cost of exposing and developing individual frames of film is nothing compared to the cost of the opportunity to do so. It's an adage you'll hear from nearly every leading underwater photographer: *Shoot as much film as you can.* The more you shoot, the more you'll learn—and the greater odds you'll get some phenomenal photos.

  This does not mean you should swim around madly, blasting away at everything in sight. Each shot you take should be deliberately composed and executed. As we discuss in the next chapter, you should also document each shot you take, so that you can learn from it later. Practice *does not* necessarily make perfect. *Perfect practice* does.

CHAPTER 4 REVIEW

1. The three most basic principles of underwater photography are: ______________________, ______ ______________ and ____________________________.

2. Wise underwater photographers separate their primary subject from similar background objects by shooting that subject ______________________ ____.

3. The best way to get your camera system into the water is to enter without the camera, then have a crewperson ___________________________________

4. The farther away your subject matter is, the less strobe light will reach it, then return to the camera. This means that subjects that are farther away require ____ (____________________________).

5. As a beginning underwater photographer it is better to set the camera to one distance, then ____ _____________________ from everything you shoot.

6. Remember that objects that appear to be (three feet) away, are actually four feet away. No problem. If it appears to be this close to your eyes, it will also appear to be that close ________ ____.

7. The most natural-looking angle for strobe light is to position it above and slightly off to one side of the camera, so that it ______________________ ____.

8. As most of the subject matter you'll shoot is taller than wider, it better fills the frame if you shoot in ______________________________.

9. Stick with one film, one camera system, one basic set of camera settings and one basic type of subject matter until ________________________ ____ ______________________________.

10. Most experienced photographers take multiple shots ____________________________________.

BUILDING ON YOUR BASIC SKILLS

5

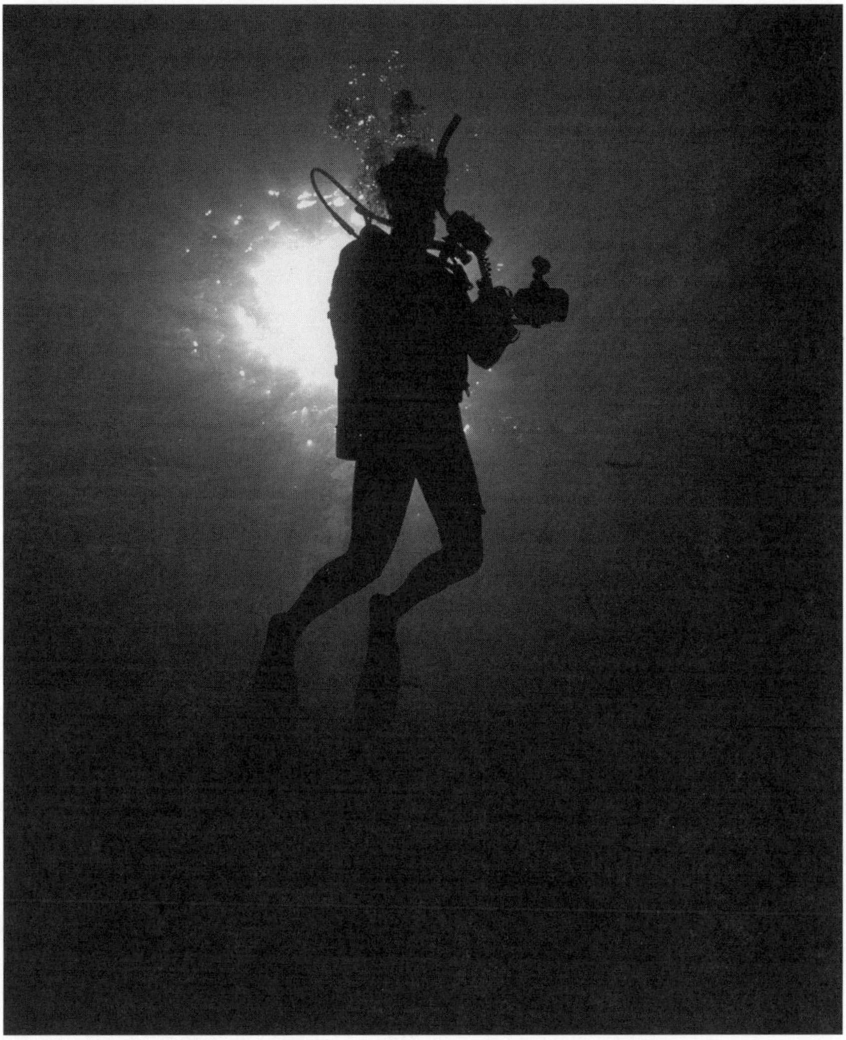

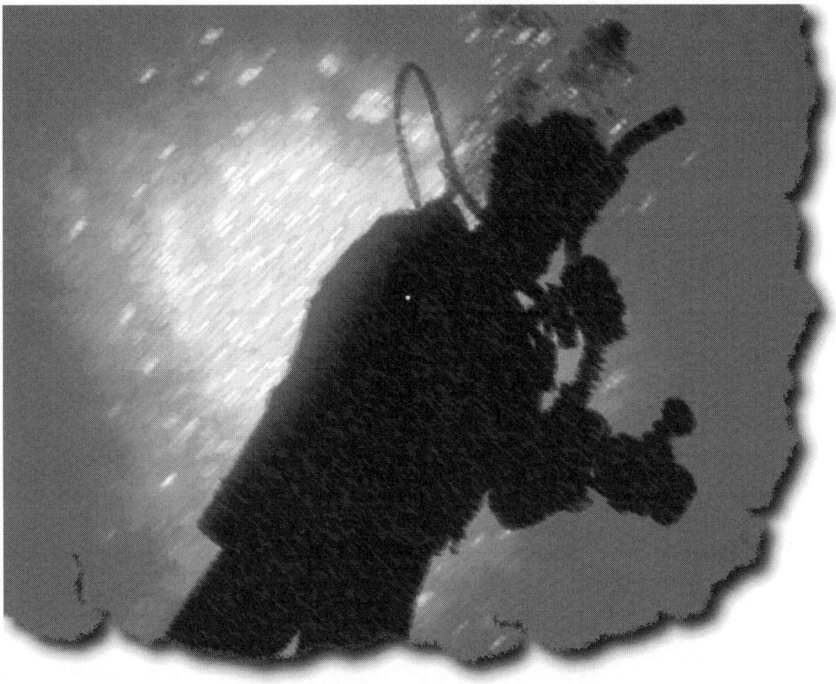

CHAPTER 5: BUILDING ON YOUR BASIC SKILLS

The primary goal of this book is to help you take your first successful underwater photos. By design, it stops at the point where most other underwater photo texts begin. If your experience with underwater photography thus far has been positive, you should plan to continue your education through additional reading, attending underwater photo seminars, workshops and clinics, and by taking additional courses.

This chapter will identify some of the opportunities available to you after you master your basic underwater photography skills. Many of these activities involve reading additional books and magazine articles, or taking additional training. They may also involve expanding your basic underwater camera system with accessory lenses and other items.

Whatever direction you choose to go, you'll find mastering these additional skills enjoyable and rewarding. Don't forget that your local SSI Dealer, and his or her staff, is standing by to help every step of the way. Take advantage of their expertise. It will make the entire experience just that much more fun.

WORKING WITH YOUR BUDDY

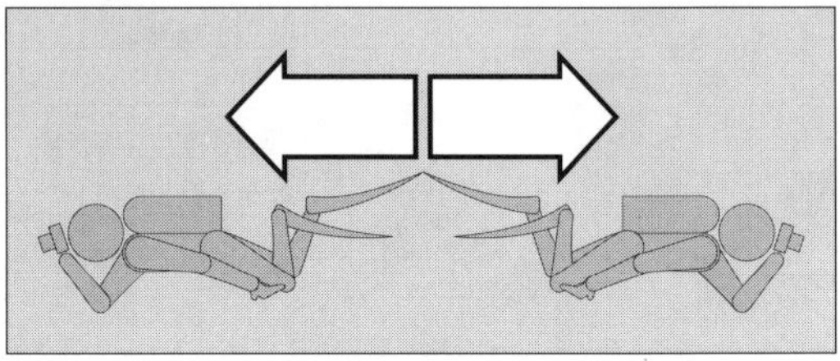

Figure 5-1 *When photographers buddy up without any plan for cooperation and support, what often results are two solo divers.*

Becoming an underwater photographer does not, by itself, justify solo diving. Yet, when an underwater photographer is paired with a diver who has different goals and ob-jectives, this is often what happens. Ironically, when two underwater photographers buddy up, the same thing can happen. Both divers look up from their work to discover they have no idea where the other is (Figure 5-1).

Both situations are unfortunate, not only from the standpoint of safety and enjoyment, but also because some of the best underwater photos result from teamwork. No buddy, no teamwork.

Dive buddies can be an important part of an underwater photographic team. They can act as safety diver, model or all-around photographic assistant. They can even be of value to one another if they both have cameras.

The key is that both divers must realize that if photography is the primary objective of either member of the team, it should be the primary objective of both members. Obviously, as a photographer, you should look for buddies who share your interest in underwater imaging, whether or not they want to actually shoot a camera.

Using Your Buddy as Safety Diver

Underwater photographers are notorious for narrowing their perception until their entire world consists of what they see through the viewfinder. Unfortunately, in the process, they can easily lose track of important factors such as depth, time and direction.

Therefore, a photographer's buddy should—at a minimum—make sure at least one member of the team is staying on top of this important, safety related information (Figure 5-2). This buddy can also act as an extra set of eyes, making sure the photographer does not accidentally bump into coral or other sensitive aquatic life. In short, a photographer's buddy is in an excellent position to act as the cameraperson's personal Dive Control Specialist, enhancing the safety and enjoyment of both members of the team.

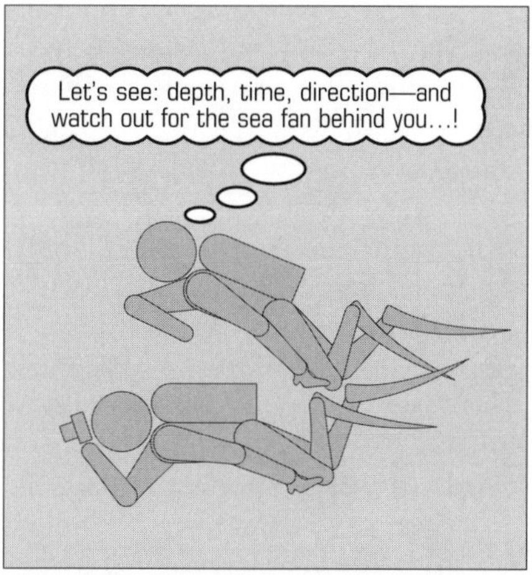

Figure 5-2 *A properly prepared buddy can act as the photographer's personal Dive Control Specialist.*

Using Your Buddy as a Model

Simply having a buddy act as safety diver is not taking full advantage of this person's potential. Among the most valuable functions a buddy can fulfill, when shooting pictures, is to act as a model.

The presence of a model greatly enhances the appeal of almost any underwater photograph (we say almost any because, obviously, human models won't fit in macro and close-up shots—and, because there are a handful of aquatic life shots that really work best on their own). Still, models add the human element to the underwater world, showing that this is not part of an alien landscape but, rather, an important part of our home planet. They help the picture tell stories of mankind's interaction with the 70 percent of our planet that is under water.

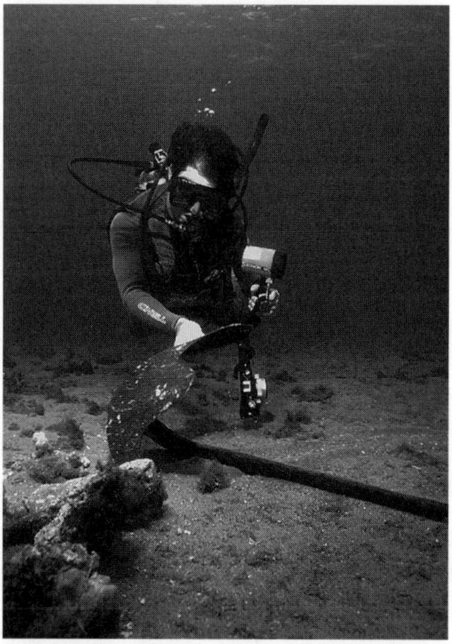

Figure 5-3 *Models give us a sense of perspective–they show us the relative size of unknown objects by posing with them.*

The presence of models also gives viewers *perspective;* it helps them tell how large or small objects are, compared with a human being (Figure 5-3). The direction a model's eyes point can direct viewers to important subject matter, calling their attention to details they might otherwise miss.

There is a wide misconception that, to be an underwater model, a person must be a certain size, shape or sex. The truth is, some of diving's most compelling photographs depict the adventures of real people under water. With reasonably up-to-date, color coordinated equipment, and mastery of a few simple techniques, almost any diver can be a good underwater model.

Information about being a better underwater model is available in books and videos. The underwater photo pros at your local SSI Dealer can help point you in their direction—as well as pass on their own personal experiences in being and working with models.

We'll give you one tip to get started: *Never have your model look directly at the camera.* Your model generally acts as your *secondary* subject. His or her job is to draw the viewer's attention to the shot's *primary* subject, which may be an artifact, animal or formation. To do this, simply have your model look at the primary subject matter. Viewers will follow his or her eyes to what you most wanted them to see (Figure 5-4).

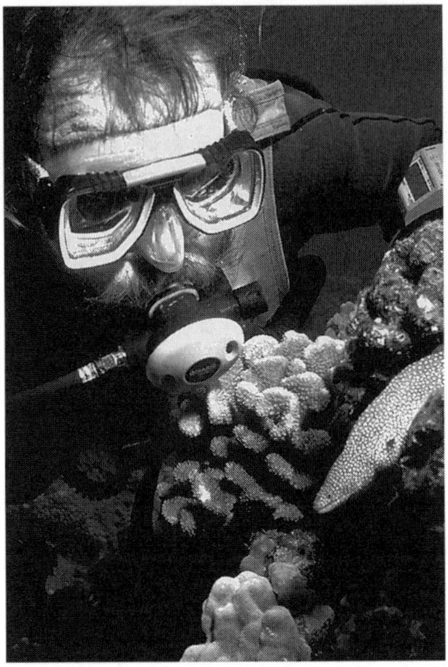

Figure 5-4 *A model's eyes can draw the viewers' attention to details they might otherwise miss.*

Using Your Buddy as a Photographic Assistant

There are several other valuable functions your buddy can perform. They can help you get camera systems and accessories in and out of the water. They can assist you in carrying equipment under water. Your buddy can provide an extra set of eyes, helping you locate up to twice as many photographic subjects as you may be able to find on your own.

What to do When Both of You Have Cameras

The idea of having a dedicated photo servant sounds appealing, but what do you do when you and your buddy both have cameras? That's easy: *You take turns* (Figure 5-5).

The problem with having both photographers shoot simultaneously is that neither can provide the important services of a photographer's buddy to one another. Also, as mentioned earlier, a buddy team of two photographers, shooting simultaneously, often ends up as two solo divers.

To prevent this, the photographers can simply take turns. One can act as cameraperson while the other fills the roll of safety diver/model/assistant. Then they can switch.

Okay, you say, *if this is true, why can't both divers simply share the same camera?* Why not, indeed? This is certainly a more equitable situation than having the non-photographer constantly subvert his or her enjoyment to meet the needs of the person with the camera. Whether it is better to have these two photographers share a single camera, or shoot different cameras, really comes to down how much film they can efficiently expose between them over the course of a single dive.

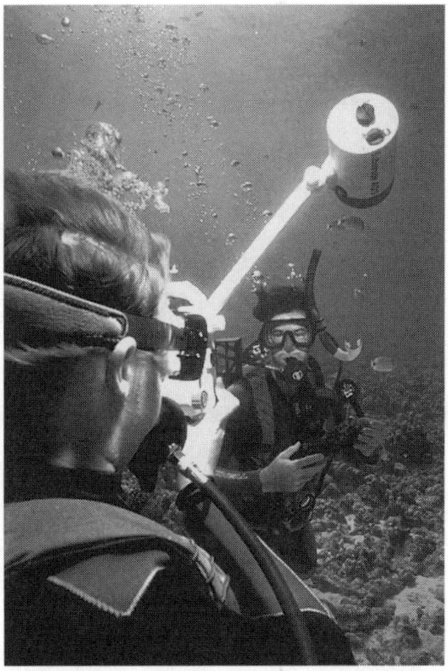

Figure 5-5 *Divers can assist each other simply by taking turns acting as photographer, model, etc.*

WHEN AND HOW TO SHOOT AQUATIC ANIMALS

In Chapter 4, we warned you not to waste time chasing solitary fish. At best, you are likely to end up with a photo of a tiny speck that, upon close examination, turns out to be the south end of a north-bound fish.

This advice is something many of you are not eager to hear. After all, the thought of getting colorful fish portraits may have been among the primary motivating factors that got you into underwater photography. Magazines and books are filled with close-ups of fish and other fast-moving animals. How do these photographers do it?

Many dive magazines provide captions listing the film, exposure settings and camera used to take these photos. Look for this information the next time you pick up such a magazine. What you will find is that, almost without exception, *the photographers use long-range, SLR macro lenses to get these shots*. As we mentioned earlier in the book, these lenses enable photographers to zoom in on fish from several feet away, without spooking them with framers or threatening them with close-in movement of the camera.

It is unrealistic to expect any underwater camera system to give you pictures it is not capable of taking. If the ability to take fish portraits is important to you, you should consider selecting or moving up to a housed SLR or Nikonos RS, with a long-range macro lens.

Understand, however, that there are many excellent shots that amphibious and disposable cameras are capable of taking. They simply do not excel at fish portraiture. Be aware, also, that having this sort of system does not exclude the possibility of getting good animal shots from time to time.

Animal Life Shots That Work

Here are several aquatic animal shots that work with a variety of cameras. Some of these shots work best with wide-angle lenses; many work best with the medium-angle lenses found on simpler cameras.

Be aware that, as a beginner, you should concentrate on stationary objects, such as coral or other formations, and shots using your buddy as a model. When you master these basic shots, however, the next step in expanding your range of skills may be to attempt some of the shots listed here.

- **Schools of Fish:** Where individual fish generally run for cover when you point a camera in their direction, schools of fish are often less timid. They will move if you stick your camera right in their midst; however, if you remain at the limit of your normal shooting distance, many schools of fish will hold their ground.

  When shooting schools of fish, try to get a montage of animals that fill your frame (Figure 5-6). Individual fish within the school will almost constantly be in motion. However, if you position yourself well, you may be able to get multiple shots of similar subject matter before the school passes you by.

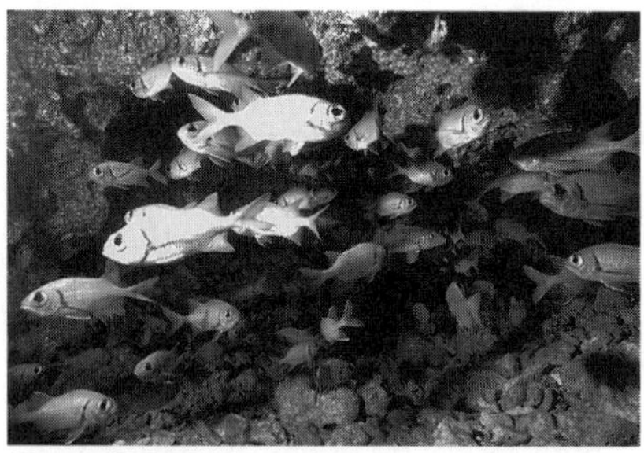

Figure 5-6 *When shooting schools of fish, try to get a montage that fills your frame.*

- **Animals in Habitats:** Some medium and larger animals like to spend time under ledges, overhangs and other protective habitats. Examples include slow-moving parrotfish, white tip reef and nurse sharks, moray eels and green sea turtles. When confronted, such animals often like to stay in these protected areas—at least long enough to give you the opportunity to get off a few shots (Figure 5-7).

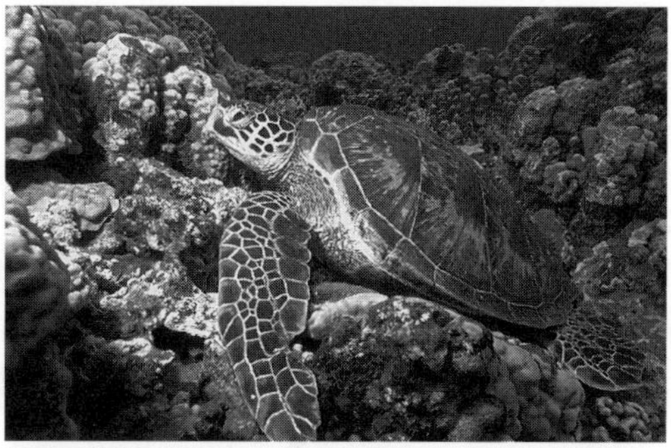

Figure 5-7 *Many larger aquatic animals will remain in their protected habitats long enough for you to get their picture.*

When shooting animals in situations such as these, you will find your standard focus and exposure settings work well. You may, however, need to angle your strobe to the side, so that its light is not blocked by an overhang.

- **Large Animal Shots:** Large aquatic animals often aren't as timid as smaller fish. If you are fortunate enough to encounter an animal like a whale shark or manatee, you may have time to get off several shots before the animal moves on (Figure 5-8). Depending on the size of the animal, you may need a wide-angle to get it entirely within your frame. Be aware that you probably will not be within strobe range. Turn your strobe off, readjust your focus and shoot in TTL mode (your strobe flash, directed in the animal's eyes, is not likely to win friends anyway).

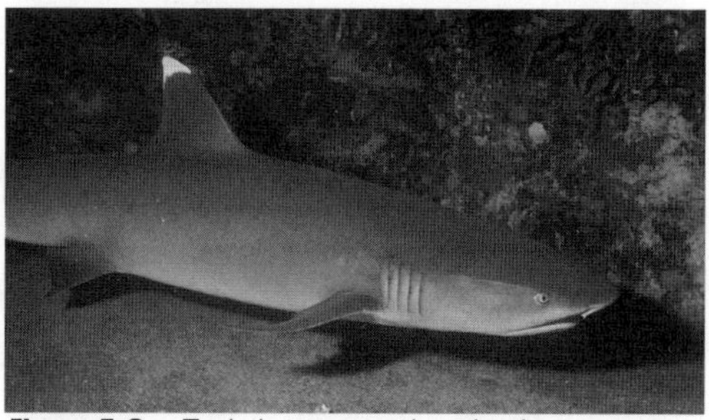

Figure 5-8 *Truly large aquatic animal encounters are rare; however, when they occur, the animal may remain around long enough for you to get several shots.*

- **Animal Interaction:** Many resort guides cultivate relationships with eels, groupers, sharks and other underwater life. They do so not only to entertain their guests, but also to provide unusual photo opportunities.

  If such a possibility is likely to present itself on a dive, your guide will alert you ahead of time. Ask how you can best take advantage of this opportunity from a photographic standpoint. Your guide will almost certainly be happy to oblige (Figure 5-9, page 102).

  Be aware that such human-animal interaction has ethical considerations. As a minimum, it should not be attempted by any but experienced professionals. You may also question whether this is a type of behavior you wish to encourage by your presence. (We'll discuss this in greater depth shortly.)

- **Shots of Opportunity:** Even though, as a beginner, you may not seek out the chance to shoot aquatic animals, there will be those opportunities that drop into your lap. Divers have turned around to find whales staring at them from within arm's reach, had elusive fish species hover right in front of them and looked up to see large sharks passing overhead. Although these opportunities are rare, you want to act quickly when they do.

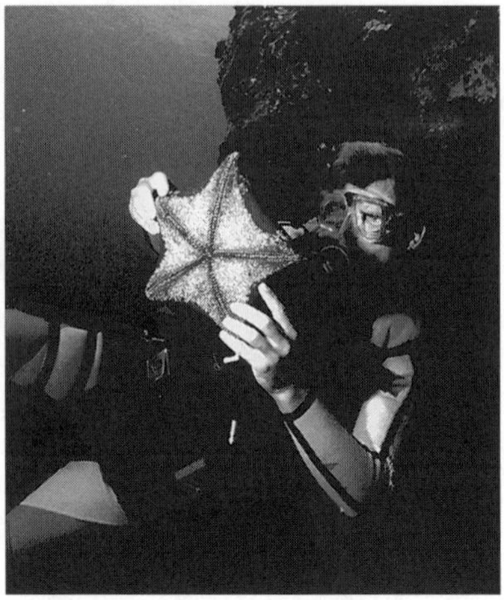

Figure 5-9 *Many resort dive guides work hard to provide good photo opportunities for guests.*

This is an additional benefit of sticking with a consistent group of distance and exposure settings. When opportunity knocks, you won't waste precious time looking up exposure settings or refocusing your camera. You can simply move to the right distance and shoot.

Your Environmental Responsibilities When Shooting Aquatic Animals

No photo is worth harming the fragile aquatic environment. This is why we have placed such an emphasis on shooting in an environmentally sound manner. Your actions when shooting aquatic life can also have severe environmental impact.

There are some fish you can attract into camera range by feeding. In so doing, however, you upset both their diet and their natural behavior. Repeatedly feeding fish at a single dive site can cause some species to flourish at the expense of others. If this feeding abruptly ends, fish who have come to depend on it may perish. Feeding some animals can make them unusually aggressive. This can lead to both animal and diver injuries.

When shooting aquatic animals, be careful not to blind them with your strobe. This is a particular hazard when shooting close ups at night. Firing a strobe directly into an animal's eyes, from just a few inches or centimetres away, can blind the animal for up to several days. A blind fish or other aquatic creature cannot defend itself from predators. It can also permanently injure itself by swimming into objects it can no longer see.

Occasionally, photographers are tempted to improve a picture's composition by manually rearranging corals, rocks and other pieces of the bottom. Doing so can easily damage these items and disturb natural habitats. It also creates photos that mislead viewers as to what the natural appearance really is.

Increasingly, dive resorts feel the pressure to offer "shark dives" and other exhibits of unnatural animal behavior. In some instances, this appears to have no adverse long-term effects—it simply is not an accurate reflection of how animals normally behave. In other instances, this type of activity may lead to environmental damage or put participating divers at risk.

As a photographer, you must ask yourself if you want to encourage this type of activity by your presence and participation—or whether you want to push for the opportunity to see natural animal behavior.

Remember, the best interaction with aquatic life is passive interaction (Figure 5-10). Chasing, threatening, cornering or feeding animals does not give the people who see your photos an accurate picture of the underwater world.

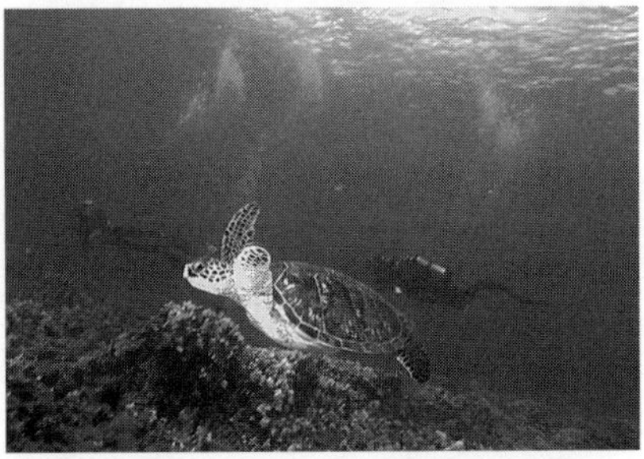

Figure 5-10 *The best interaction with aquatic life is passive interaction, in which divers do nothing to alter animals' natural behavior.*

BRACKETING SHOTS

The TTL circuitry found in most underwater camera systems frees beginning underwater photographers from having to worry about complex exposure calculations, and lets them concentrate on correct distance to subject, shooting angle and composition. It is surprisingly accurate. It is not, however, perfect.

Sometimes, environments with bright, sunlit areas and dark shadows can fool TTL circuitry, as can models with light faces and dark suits. At other times, the technically correct exposure is not the most aesthetically pleasing.

For this reason, wise underwater photographers often "buy insurance" by *bracketing* their exposures. Bracketing is so simple a procedure that your Underwater Photography Instructor may have you practice it from the very beginning.

What is Bracketing?

When you bracket, you take at least three shots of the same subject. On your first shot, you either use your TTL system to take exactly the exposure the camera thinks is best, or use equivalent manual exposure settings. This way, if your first shot is the only shot you get to take, it will be the one with the greatest likelihood of being shot at the right exposure.

On your subsequent shots, you alternate between letting more light and less light into the camera than the metering system allows. This way, if the camera's metering system is wrong, you increase the odds of having at least one exposure you find pleasing to look at (Figure 5-11).

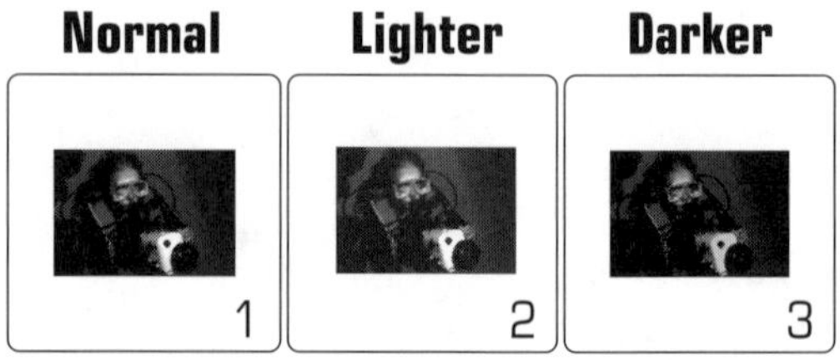

Figure 5-11 *By bracketing photos, you increase the likelihood of getting at least one acceptable exposure.*

When and Why Can Bracketing be Beneficial?

Bracketing can be beneficial whenever you have time to take multiple shots of the same subject. To bracket effectively, however, you must be using a camera system that allows it, and you generally must be using *reversal* (slide) film. As we mentioned in Chapter 1, print film is so forgiving (has greater *latitude*) that you would have to under- or overexpose by several *exposure values* (the equivalent of an *f*-stop, or doubling or halving shutter speeds) to notice an appreciable difference.

Determining if Your Camera System Allows Bracketing

Not all camera systems allow bracketing (Figure 5-12). Here is how to determine if your camera will enable you to bracket exposures.

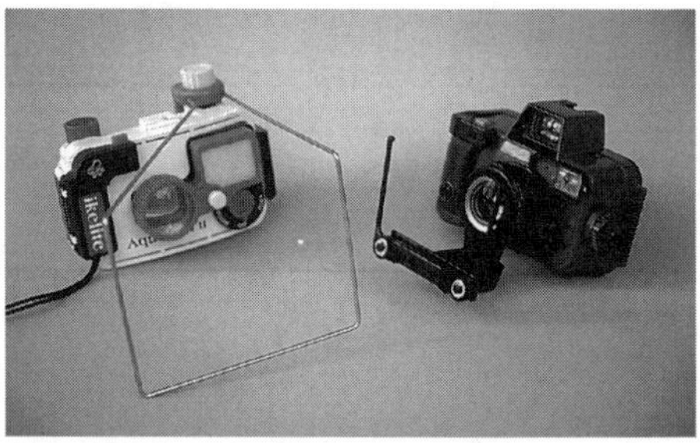

Figure 5-12 *Not all underwater camera systems allow you to bracket exposures.*

Disposable cameras have no exposure settings; therefore, no bracketing is possible. Additionally, the ISO 400 print film they use has such tremendous latitude that, even if you could change exposure settings, you would not likely notice any difference. On the other hand, this extreme latitude eliminates much of the need to bracket—albeit at the expense of coarser grain and less color saturation.

Sea & Sea cameras shoot only in TTL mode. You can put Sea & Sea strobes in a manual, full-power mode, while the camera itself selects shutter speeds. By doing this while varying strobe-to-subject distance, you may achieve some variation in exposures. Doing so successfully, however, requires complex calculations, and is not recommended for beginners.

You can bracket with the Nikonos V in a variety of ways, if shooting manually. Even if shooting in TTL mode, as most Instructors recommend beginners do, there is an easy and effective way to bracket. We'll cover it shortly.

Most modern SLR cameras and the Nikonos RS have very sophisticated, yet easy-to-use ways to bracket shots. We will also cover these next.

Techniques for Bracketing

When controlling exposures manually, you can bracket by changing *f*-stops or shutter speeds, or varying strobe-to-subject distance. None of these methods work, however, when shooting in TTL mode; the camera's internal circuitry automatically compensates for such changes. Therefore, to bracket while in TTL mode, you must control how much light enters the camera some other way.

To bracket when shooting a Nikonos V in TTL mode, you can fool the camera by changing the ISO setting, telling it that you are using a film that is either faster or slower than you really are. For example, when shooting with ISO 100 reversal film, you can bracket by taking one shot with the ISO dial set at *100,* one with it set a *50* and one with it set at *200* (Figure 5-13). By so doing, you take: a shot that the camera's metre says is right on the money; a shot in which twice as much light hits the film; and one in which only half as much light hits the film.

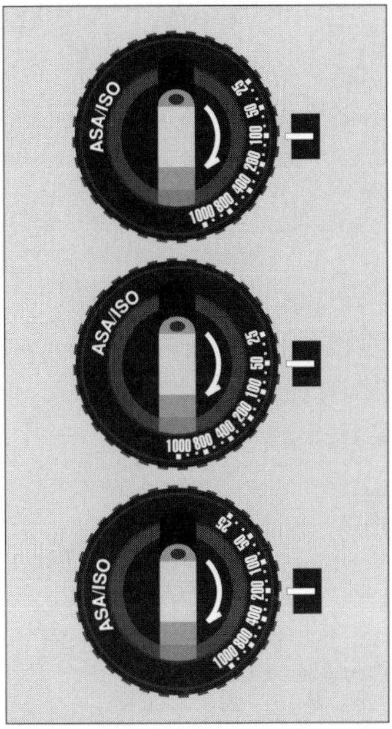

Figure 5-13 *You can bracket while shooting Nikonos V cameras in TTL mode by altering ISO settings between shots.*

This same method works with many SLR cameras—providing your housing allows you to change ISO settings under water. A number of SLR cameras, and the Nikonos RS, also have an easy-to-use *exposure compensation* dial. This enables you to intentionally over- or underexpose film by up to three *EV* (exposure values).

Many of the latest SLRs are even programmable, allowing you to automatically take a series of three to seven shots in which the exposure values change in units of one-third to one-and-a-half EV with each successive shot. Before you get carried away with this awesome technology, however, be aware that many of the world's best underwater photographers now feel that the metering systems on these SLRs are so advanced, the average diver may have little to gain by bracketing.

SHOOTING SILHOUETTES

Silhouettes are the kind of shots that no underwater photographer is likely to base his or her entire portfolio on. Still, because they are so easy to take, most photographers have several in their collection. Whether in slide shows or photo albums, silhouettes are good mood-setting and transitional shots. They help you move the story from one setting to another.

What are Silhouettes?

Silhouettes are shots in which an object, such as a diver or large aquatic animal, is outlined by the sun (Figure 5-14). These are dramatic shots. You often see them on brochure, book and magazine covers.

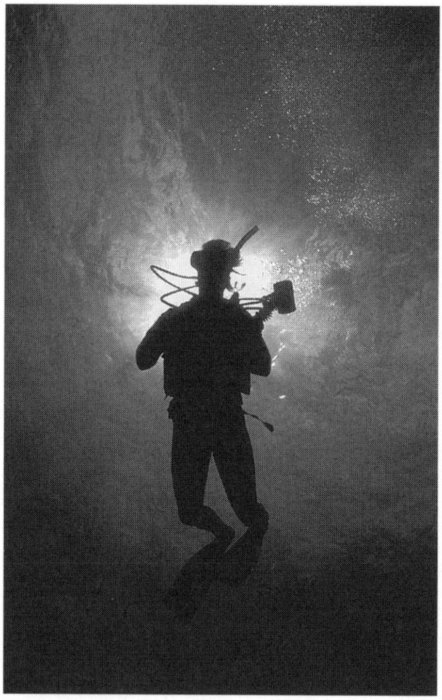

Figure 5-14 *Silhouette.*

How Does Shooting Silhouettes Differ?

Silhouettes are among the few shots you are likely to take without using your strobe. Because your primary subject will probably be well beyond strobe range, there is little your strobe can do, other than confuse your camera's TTL circuitry.

Obviously, without strobe light, your silhouette will be largely monochromatic. That's okay. A silhouette is a study in contrasts, not in colors.

Shooting silhouettes adheres to the principles *Get Low* and *Shoot Up.* It is the one type of shot, however, where it does not matter whether your subject is just out of arm's reach—only that it fills an adequate part of the frame. Most silhouettes are shot at distances of 10-20 feet (3-6 metres).

Techniques for Shooting the Best Silhouettes

Taking silhouettes are surprisingly easy. Here is what to do:

- **Turn Your Strobe Off:** This will enable your camera's TTL circuitry to regain control over shutter speed (on most cameras, using a TTL strobe locks your shutter speed at 1/90th, 1/100th or 1/125th of a second).
- **Get Your Model in Place:** Silhouettes of large aquatic animals, such as manta rays, dolphins and whale sharks, are entirely shots of opportunity. You are far more likely to take your first silhouettes of a model. Direct your model into a position directly between you and the sun. Have him or her hover horizontally. You may have to move a little yourself to keep your model in line with the sun.
- **Re-set Your Focus:** Use your best estimate of the distance between you and the model. This setting is not likely to be as accurate as when you shoot close up. No problem. At this greater distance, you also have far greater depth of field.
- **Meter Your Shot:** Look in your viewfinder and see what shutter speed your camera is selecting, based on available light. Open your aperture until the selected shutter speed is 1/250th of a second, or faster (Figure 5-15). This faster shutter speed may actually freeze the rays of light in your shot, heightening the drama.

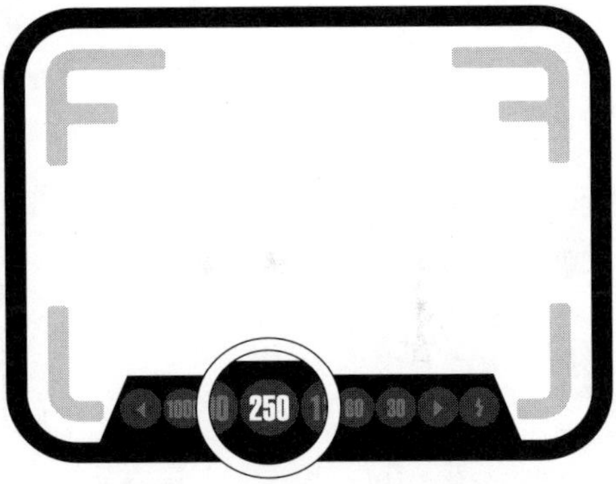

Figure 5-15 *By shooting at shutter speeds of 1/250th of a second or higher, you may be able to capture the sun's rays in your silhouette shots.*

- **Take Multiple Shots:** As with any type of underwater shot, you can't assume that your first exposure will come out perfectly. You may also want to experiment by changing the position of yourself or your model, or by bracketing.
- **Remember to Restore Your Settings:** You don't want to go back to your normal shooting mode without first turning your strobe back on, resetting your focal distance and, if necessary, re-setting your aperture.

CLOSE-UP AND MACRO UNDERWATER PHOTOGRAPHY

Among the most dramatic of all underwater photos are those taken at extremely close range. We've all seen photos in which coral polyps, arrow crabs, flamingo tongues and neon gobies appear many times their actual size (Figures 5-16a & b). These are close-up and macro shots.

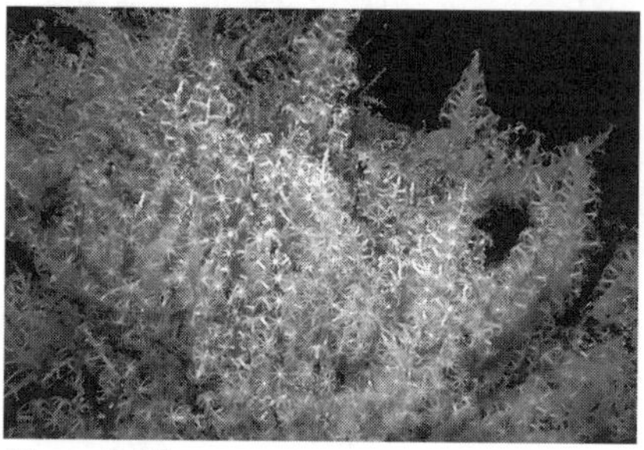

Figure 5-16a

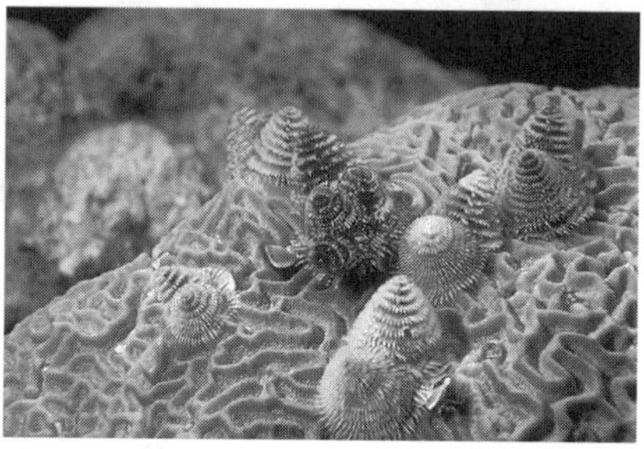

Figure 5-16b

Macro and close-up shots are those taken at very close range.

With just the use of simple accessories, close-up and macro shots can be easy to take. In fact, macro photography with am-phibious cameras is so easy that, if there is considerable macro subject matter in the area where you will be learning, your Underwater Photography Instructor may start you off by taking macro shots rather than shots using standard lenses (Figure 5-17).

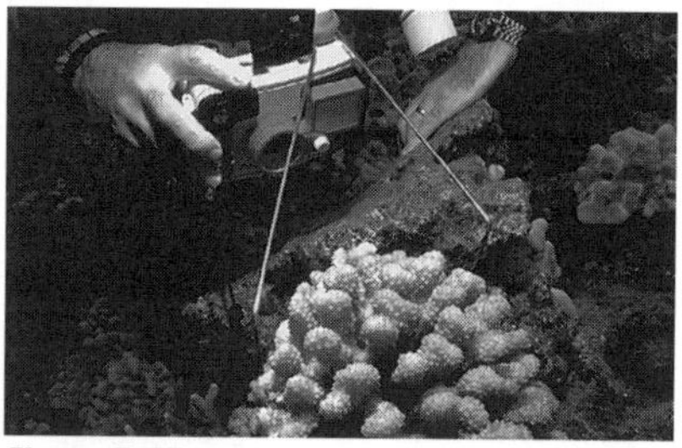

Figure 5-17 *Macro photography is so easy, your Instructor may have you begin by shooting this type of photo exclusively.*

What are Close-up and Macro Photography?

Close-up photos are generally those taken within 12–18 inches (30–45 centimetres) of the camera lens. The resulting images appear on film at roughly one-fifth their actual size.

Macro photos are usually taken much closer than this. When measured on a 35mm negative or slide, the resulting images can be anywhere from one-fifth to twice their actual size. Reproduced as a standard photographic print, they may appear life size or larger. Projected on a slide screen, the images will appear dozens of times their actual size.

What are the Benefits and Drawbacks of Close-up and Macro Photography?

Close-up and macro photos give us the opportunity to examine aquatic life far more closely, and for a longer time than we can in person. They are vivid photos, rich in color and texture. They do a wonderful job of impressing divers and non-divers alike. Best of all, they are very easy to shoot.

The only significant drawback to close-up and macro photography is that it requires either special lenses, extension tubes or add-on diopters. If you are shooting a Nikonos with an extension tube, or an SLR with a macro lens, you will not be able to remove them underwater to take other kinds of photos. This means that if a large aquatic animal swims by, or some other great standard or wide-angle lens opportunity drops in your lap, you will not be able to take advantage of it.

What Special Equipment Will I Need for Close-up and Macro Photography?

Most underwater camera systems you can buy are capable of taking close-ups. All are capable of taking macro shots. You will, however, need some specialized accessory equipment.

- **Housed Disposable Cameras:** Ikelite makes an inexpensive macro attachment for their Aquashot disposable camera housing. It consists, in part, of a diopter (accessory magnifying lens) that attaches to the outside of the housing. This fits over the standard lens port. Attached to this is a framer, designed to help photographers center their subject and shoot it from the proper distance. Also built in to this attachment is a *diffuser*, which softens the beam of the camera's built-in flash, and spreads it over an area wide enough to cover the framer (Figure 5-18).

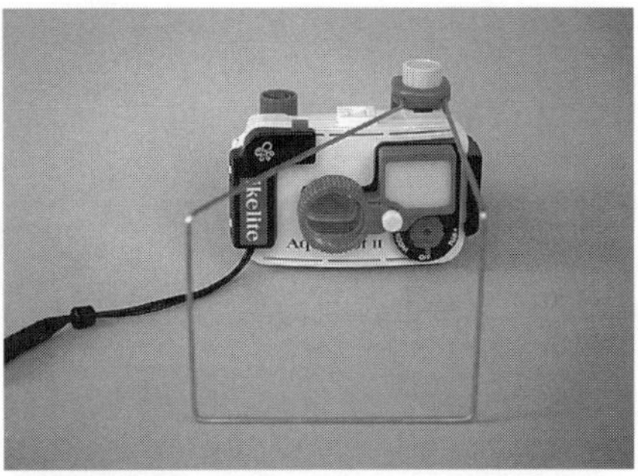

Figure 5-18 *Ikelite Aquashot II with macro attachment.*

  The Aquashot macro kit may be attached or removed under water. This means you can take both macro and standard-lens shots on the same dive.

- **Sea & Sea Cameras:** The Sea & Sea Motormarine II and Seamaster Pro cameras come with a built-in close-up lens. By switching the focus selector switch to the CU (close-up) position (Figure 5-19), you can focus on objects roughly one to two feet (30–60 centimetres) away.

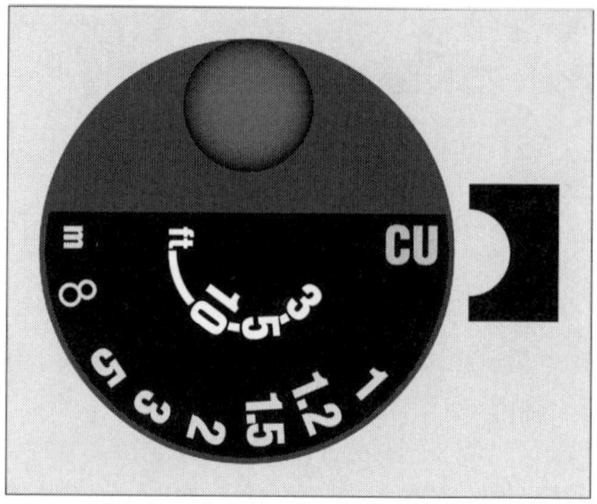

Figure 5-19 *Sea & Sea cameras have a special close-up setting built in.*

Sea & Sea also makes macro lenses and framers for these cameras, with reproduction ratios of 1:2 and 1:3. Like the Ikelite Aquashot system, both lenses are external diopters, meaning you can attach and remove them under water.

- **Nikonos Cameras:** Nikon makes a close-up kit that works with several Nikonos lenses. These kits include an external diopter, a support arm, a framer wand and separate framers for the 28mm, 35mm and 80mm lenses. The kit may be attached or removed under water.

For macro work, both Nikon and other manufacturers make extension tubes for the 28mm and 35mm Nikonos lenses (Figure 5-20). These extension tubes go between the lens and the camera body, meaning that you can neither attach nor remove them under water. While this may be a drawback in terms of convenience, it helps ensure sharper and clearer images than it is possible to obtain with external diopters or accessory lenses.

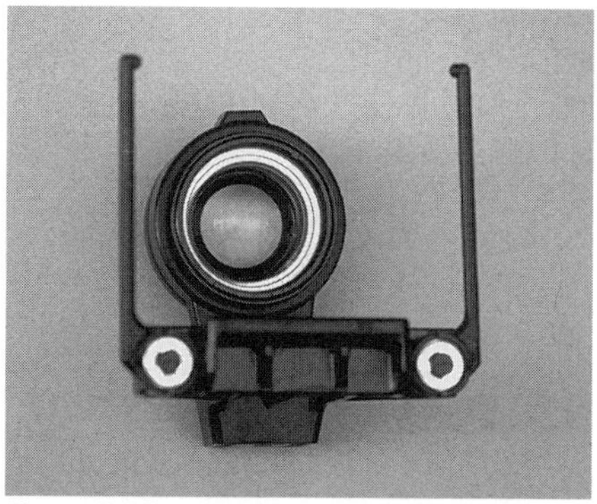

Figure 5-20 *A wide variety of extension tubes, diopters and framers are available for both Sea & Sea and Nikonos amphibious cameras.*

Nikonos extension tubes are available for 1:3, 1:2, 1:1 and 2:1 reproduction ratios. Each has its own framer.

- **Housed SLR Cameras:** Special macro lenses are available for most SLR cameras in focal lengths from 50mm to 105mm. Longer focal lengths mean higher reproduction ratios—that is, able to see smaller objects.

A 50mm macro lens is very different from the 50mm lens that comes with most consumer SLRs. It is a longer lens, with a narrow angle of coverage. It can focus on tiny objects just a few inches or centimetres from the camera—or on small-to-medium size objects up to a yard (or metre) or more away.

Macro lenses with longer focal lengths, such as a 105mm lens, can capture very tiny objects. They do not have as great a range, however. Most SLR photographers prefer to use macro lenses in the 50mm to 60mm range.

As with all macro and close-up photography, long focal lengths mean very narrow depth of field. Although SLR macro lenses do not require external framers, they can be difficult for some divers to focus manually. As mentioned in Chapter 1, it took the advent of reliable autofocus mechanisms to make macro photography practical for many SLR owners.

To use macro lenses, SLR housings require a special port. This port has a flat surface; hence the name: *flat port*. Flat ports tend to have long barrels, to house the long macro lenses (Figure 5-21).

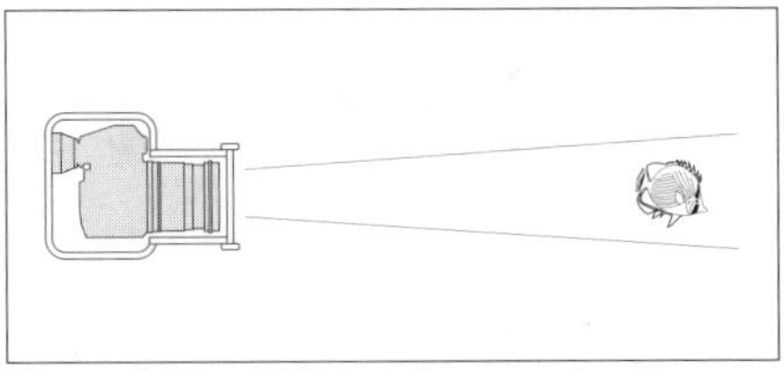

Figure 5-21 *SLR housings require the use of special flat ports when shooting long macro lenses.*

SLR macro and close-up photography enjoys two distinct advantages over macro and close-up photography using extension tubes, external diopters and framers. First, the absence of framers and the ability to shot from farther away means you are less likely to spook fish and other fast-moving animals. Second, SLR macro lenses enable you to shoot objects in a variety of size ranges. If you want to capture something small, get close to it; if you want something large, move farther back. In contrast, with framer-based systems, you are limited to shooting objects the size of the framer.

On the other hand, SLR macro equipment costs more. It is also considerably bulkier to travel with and to use under water.

Basic Close-up and Macro Techniques

Although close-up and macro photography are relatively easy, procedures vary from one camera system to another. You will need to, as a minimum, read a book or watch a video dedicated to the exact procedures you should follow with your system. Better still, learn from an SSI Underwater Photography Instructor who is familiar with your type of camera and macro set up.

If you are using a framer-based system, it will be vital to not only center your subject in the framer, but to keep that subject within the plane of the framer. Your depth-of-field with any type of macro or close-up system will be minimal—often no more than a finger's width. If your subject is not within the plane of the framer, it will be out of focus (Figure 5-22).

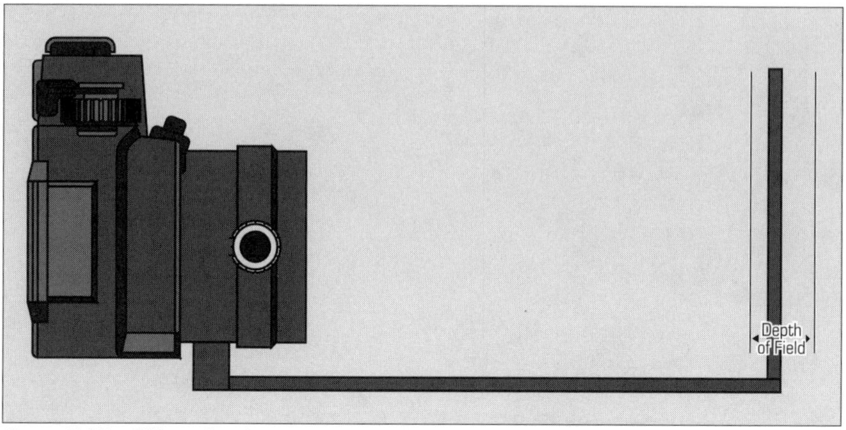

Figure 5-22 *When shooting macro, your depth of field is barely greater than the framer.*

Among the many ways you can experiment with macro and close-up photography is to vary strobe position. Techniques such as *top lighting, side lighting* and *back-lighting* produce a variety of effects (Figure 5-23).

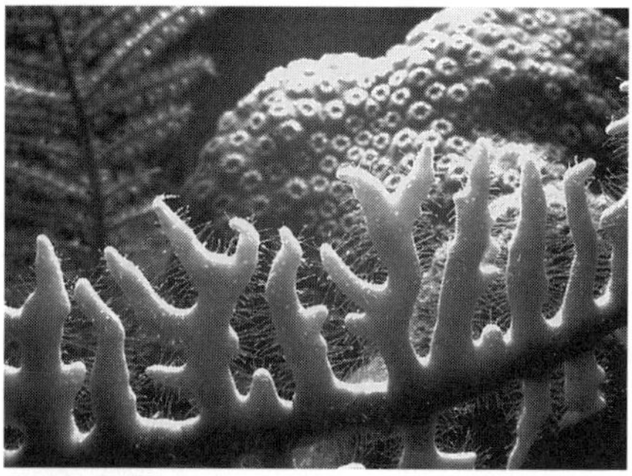

Figure 5-23 *Top, side and back lighting produce a variety of effects.*

You will discover that night time is perhaps the best time for macro photography. This is when coral polyps come out to feed, and there may be other macro subjects available that you cannot find as readily during the day. One thing you do not want to do, however, is to stick your camera system directly in the face of sleeping or slow moving fish. As mentioned earlier, this will only blind the fish, making them vulnerable to injury or predation.

WIDE-ANGLE UNDERWATER PHOTOGRAPHY

It is tough to say whether wide-angle photographs are the most popular type of underwater photography. One thing, however, is without question: Wide-angle photographs are diving's *most published* form of underwater imagery.

Whether you are seeking to break into publication, or are simply seeking to capture what are arguably the most dramatic of all forms of underwater photography, wide-angle shots are almost certainly something you will want to move up to.

What is Wide-Angle Photography?

A wide-angle photograph is any picture taken with a lens whose angle of coverage, under water, is greater than 60 degrees (Figure 5-24). This includes amphibious camera lenses with focal lengths of 24mm or less, and housed SLR lenses with focal lengths of 28mm or less.

A 60-degree field of view is what most of us can see under water with our masks on. We refer to lenses that can see nearly as much as *medium-angle* lenses. Any lens capable of seeing more than our eyes can at the same distance is a *wide-angle* lens.

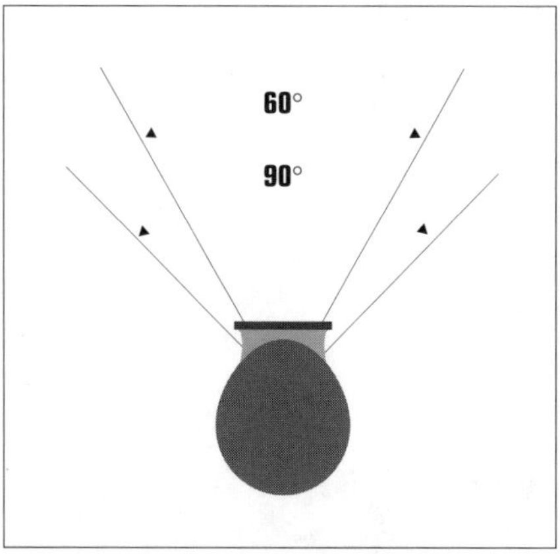

Figure 5-24 *Our eyes have a 60-degree field of view under water; we categorize lenses that have a wider angle of acceptance than this as wide-angle lenses.*

What are the Benefits and Drawbacks of Wide-Angle Photography?

Wide-angle photography offers several advantages. It offers us seemingly limitless depth of field. At common *f*-stops, this depth of field puts everything from just outside arm's reach to infinity in razor-sharp focus.

Wide-angle photography makes everything look farther away. In the process, it can make murky water look clear. Wide-angle lenses gather more light. This improves color saturation and allows us to shoot at higher *f*-stops.

Additionally, wide-angle lenses enable us to shoot panoramic landscapes we could not otherwise capture. Because they create the illusion of objects being farther away than they really are, wide-angle lenses can make it appear our strobe light also reaches farther (Figure 5-25).

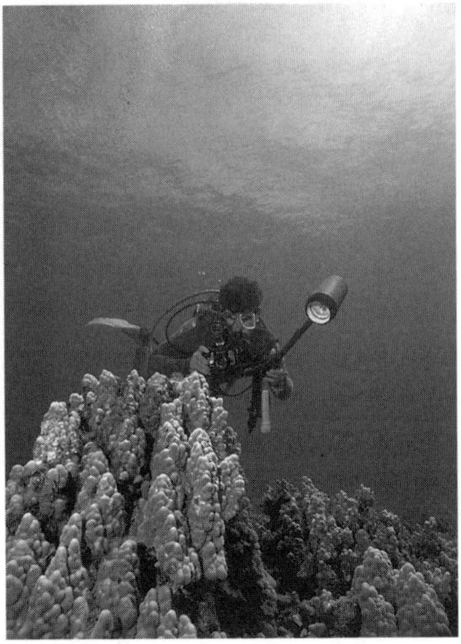

Figure 5-25 *Wide-angle lenses can create the illusion that our strobe light reaches farther than it actually can.*

What are the drawbacks of wide-angle photography? Increased cost is first on the list. Wide-angle lenses for Sea & Sea and Nikonos cameras typically exceed the cost of the camera body—in some cases by a mar-gin of nearly 2:1. SLR wide-angle lenses also cost more than medium-angle lenses—but not by so wide a margin.

Wide-angle lenses suffer from a phenomena called *forced perspective*. If a model extends a hand or leg toward the camera, a wide-angle lens will grossly exaggerate this, distorting the model's image to inhuman proportions.

It is difficult for some photographers to accept the fact wide-angle lenses see more than they do. As a result, their subject matter may be lost in the center of the picture, amidst scenery the photographer didn't even realize was there.

What Special Equipment Will I Need for Wide-Angle Photography?

To take wide-angle photographs you need a wide-angle lens. (You knew that—right?) For amphibious cameras, an external viewfinder, matched to your lens, is essential. If your wide-angle lens' angle of coverage exceeds that of your present strobe, you will need to either add a diffuser, add a second strobe of similar size, or move up to a larger strobe (Figure 5-26).

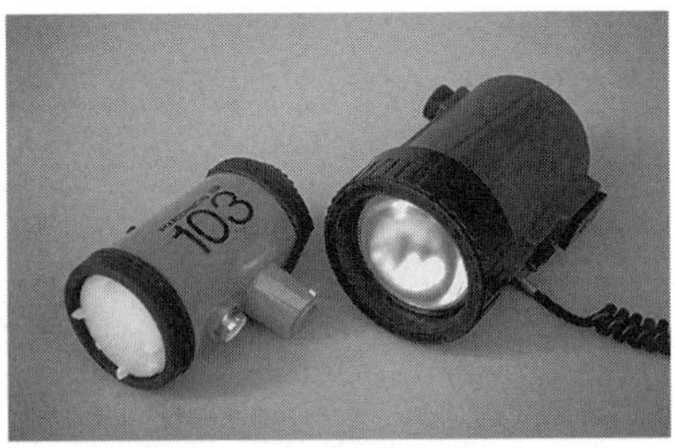

Figure 5-26 *To ensure a proper angle of coverage for wide-angle photography, you may need to add a diffuser to your strobe or move up to a larger model.*

Many photographic experts recommend sticking with a small strobe for wide-angle photography in clear ocean water. Under these conditions, you use strobes only for *fill-in flash;* ambient light is your primary light source. If you stick with a smaller strobe, however, its angle of coverage must still approach that of the lens.

Wide-angle lenses are available for amphibious cameras and housed SLRs. There are presently no wide-angle options for housed disposables.

Sea & Sea makes 16mm and 20mm wide-angle lenses for the Motor-marine II and Seamaster Pro cameras. They also make a 20mm lens for the MX-10. These lenses go on the outside of the camera's primary lens, and may be attached and removed under water. This flexibility enables divers to take wide-angle, close-up and macro shots on the same dive, providing they have the right accessories. Sea & Sea also makes a 16mm external lens that attaches to the outside of the standard 35mm Nikonos lens.

Both Nikon and Sea & Sea make 15mm and 20mm dedicated lenses for Nikonos cameras. Aqua Vision makes a housing that allows SLR wide-angle lenses to be used with Nikonos cameras. Sea & Sea makes a 12mm fisheye lens that can also be used with the Nikonos. These are all dedicated lenses; they cannot be attached or removed under water. The trade-off is that dedicated lenses offer better quality optics and provide sharper pictures than external lenses can.

Nikon also makes a 28mm lens for the Nikonos. Some divers consider this a wide-angle lens as well. In reality, its 60-degree angle of coverage matches what the human eye sees. This lens costs slightly more than the "standard" 35mm lens, but offers nearly twice as much depth of field (Figure 5-27). Not only does this lead to more in-focus shots, the fact it so closely matches what divers see with their eyes means fewer mistakes are caused by being too close or too far from the subject.

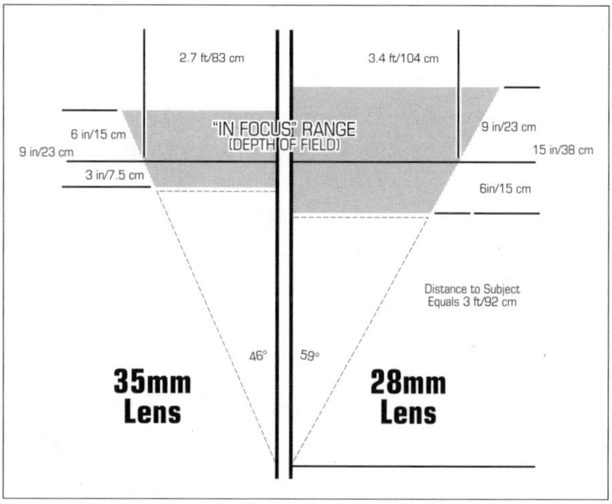

Figure 5-27 *The Nikonos 28mm lens offers almost twice the depth of field as the "standard" 35mm lens.*

There are a wide variety of wide-angle lenses available for housed SLR cameras. Most divers use a 20mm, fixed-focal-length lens for wide-angle, SLR underwater photographs. Its angle of coverage, 94 degrees, is equal to that of a 15mm Nikonos lens.

Using a wide-angle lens with a housed SLR requires a *dome port.* This port's curved surface corrects for refraction. It creates a *virtual image* of what the camera sees approximately 12 inches (30 centimetres) in front of the port (Figure 5-28). By focusing on this virtual image once, nearly everything you want to shoot will be in razor sharp focus for the balance of the dive.

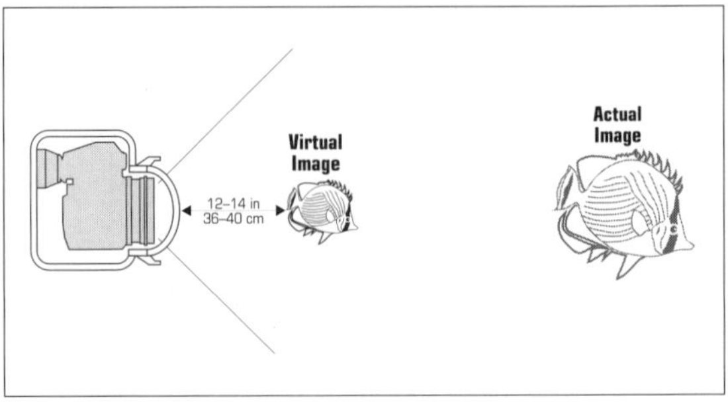

Figure 5-28 *Dome ports create a virtual image just in front of the camera's lens.*

Basic Wide-Angle Techniques

As with close-up and macro photography you will need to read a book or watch a video dedicated to the exact procedures you should follow with your system. And, again, learning from an SSI Underwater Photography Instructor who is familiar with your type of camera is best.

The most basic challenge in dealing with wide-angle photography is the fact the lens sees more than you do. You must compose your shots through the viewfinder. If you do so with your eyes, you will end up with shots in which your subject matter appears as a tiny speck in the middle of the picture (Figure 5-29).

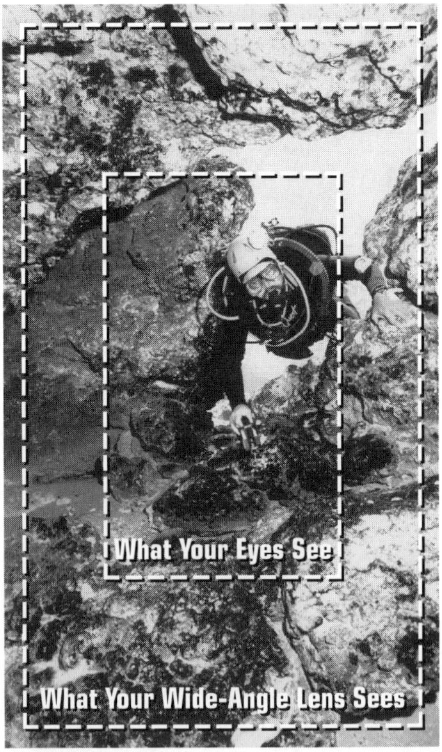

Figure 5-29 *If you do not compose your wide-angle shots through the viewfinder, you may end up with photos in which your primary subject matter is just a speck in the middle.*

Wide-angle lenses often fool the less sophisticated metering systems found in amphibious cameras. For this reason, experienced photographers often use an external light meter and set exposures manually when taking wide angle photos. Because ambient light, not strobe light, is usually the primary light source in wide-angle photography, you will have to learn to do the mental mathematics for balancing fill-in flash against available light. This is covered in more detail in advanced underwater photography texts.

The light meters in older SLR cameras may suffer from the same limitations as amphibious cameras when it comes to wide-angle shots. Newer SLRs employ *matrix metering,* a sophisticated system that measures ambient light in up to five or more segments of the frame. These work well with wide-angle lenses.

USING A PHOTO LOG

Imagine how difficult going to school would have been if, after taking a test, you never got to see which answers you got wrong, or what the correct answers were. This is very much what it's like to shoot underwater photos without keeping a log.

What is a Photo Log?

A photo log is a means of recording all the experiences that will make future photos turn out better. It's a record of how, when and where you learned the lessons that keep improving your photos. It's a handy reference to the experiments that worked, and those that didn't. In short, it can be whatever you make it.

Why is it Important?

Earlier we said that, while the direct cost of exposing film is cheap, the opportunity to shoot that film may not be. Obviously, repeating the same mistakes can be painful and expensive. Being able to avoid mistakes by referring to a photo log can save time and money.

How do You Keep a Photo Log?

This is highly personal. Because each photographer has different needs, each photographer's log book—although similar in design—may differ somewhat in function. The SSI Photo Log that accompanies this book has a designed-in flexibility that enables you to use it in a variety of ways (Figure 5-30, page 119). Exactly how you do so is up to you. Here are some generalizations that may help.

- **Begin the Logging Process Under Water:** In the days before TTL photography, it was common for photographers to carry slates that allowed them to record the *f*-stop, shutter speed

SCUBA SCHOOLS SSI® INTERNATIONAL

SPECIALTY Diver

UNDERWATER PHOTOGRAPHY SLATE

Directions: On the first line, list the camera settings you normally use for most of the pictures you take. If you alter these settings for one or more frames, record the new settings next to the appropriate frame number. Use the "Comments" column to record anything from shot location to subject or technique used. For an example of how to use this slate, see the SSI *Underwater Photography* manual.

Frame Number	Distance to Subject	*f*-stop (Aperture)	Shutter Speed	ISO Setting	Comments
	3	8	A	100	⬅ Standard settings for this roll, unless otherwise indicated for individual frames
1					EAGLE REEF SPONGE
2	4	5.6			SEA FAN
3				100	MIXED FORMATION (BRACKETED)
4				50	·
5				200	·
6					ANGEL FISH
7					·
8	4				·
9	4				· (NOT WORTH EFFORT!)
10	3.5			100	SUE W/CORAL (BRACKETED)
11	3.5			50	·
12	3.5			200	·
13	2	11			SPONGE (FIND OUT WHAT KIND)

...continues on back

Figure 5-30 *A photo log is a record of how, where and when you learned the lessons that make you a better photographer.*

and focal distance for each shot they took. Many successful underwater photographers still do this.

Today, however, TTL photography has eliminated the need for beginners to constantly change exposure settings. In fact, if you follow the advice of most photo pros, you'll take each shot using a consistent group of settings, until your skills develop to the point where you are ready to experiment.

This doesn't mean that you should not record what you do under water. If your basic settings remain the same from shot to shot, what you should record are the things you did differently. Did you change camera or strobe angle? Did you shoot familiar subject matter from a different direction? What new technique did you try that you want to repeat if it works—and avoid if it fails? The SSI Photo Slate, which also accompanies this text, enables you to record this information, along with specific information on f-stop, shutter speed, focal distance and film speed, if these settings vary from your norm.

Key your notes to your frame counter, so that you know the reef, wreck or dive site at which a particular shot was taken. If unusual lighting forces you to change an *f*-stop, write it down. If you shoot a silhouette, note the shutter speed the camera selected. If you bracket shots, list when and how you fooled the camera. This will give you a record of which shots represent variations from your standard settings (Figure 5-31).

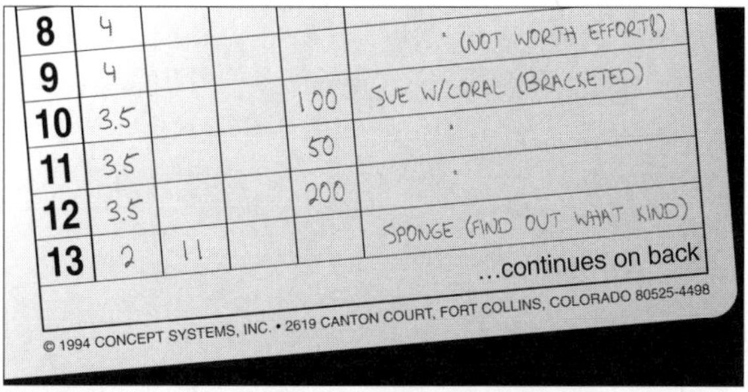

Figure 5-31 *Your logging process should begin under water, on your slate. Note where you took each shot, and what steps you took that differed from your "normal" shooting methods.*

- **Get the Where and When Down:** The SSI Photo Log that accompanies this book has a section to record where and when you shot every roll of film you take ("If this is Bonaire, it must be March of '95…"). You may at times travel to places where the availability of only certain types of overnight developing require that you use a different film. Note it in your log—it will be helpful when you return. The pages of this section also allow you to transfer data directly from your SSI Photo Slate, so that you can erase it and use it for the next set of dives.

- **Departmentalize:** Because much of what you keep in your photo log depends on personal preference, the SSI Photo Log contains several blank pages you may customize however you choose. We recommend using some of these pages to document every experiment or out-of-the ordinary technique you try. When the film comes back, you can transfer the results to the pages you label, *Experiments That Worked, Experiments That Didn't Work* and *Worthy of Further Experimentation.*

  You may want to use another page to keep a *Wish List.* What is it you discovered that would have been nice to have this time—and that you want to make certain you have next time? This can be anything from plastic tape and waterproof markers, to a wider lens or external viewfinder.

- **Inventory:** A very important section of the SSI Photo Log are the pages that enable you to maintain a record of the makes, models and serial numbers of every piece of photo equipment you own. This tells you exactly what is it you'll need to replace if you lose one or more items. There is also space to record when and where you had each item serviced. Be aware that this list is only of value if you keep it separate from your photo equipment—preferably with a back-up photocopy in a secure place at home.

CHAPTER 5 REVIEW

1. Dive buddies can be an important part of an underwater photographic team. They can act as safety diver, model or ______________________ ______________________________________.

2. The presence of ____________________ greatly enchances the appeal of almost any underwater photograph.

3. Your model generally acts as your ____________ ________. His or her job is to draw the viewer's attention to the shot's ____________________.

4. If the ability to take fish portraits is important to you, you should consider selecting or moving up to a housed SLR or Nikonos RS, with a ________ ______________________________________.

5. Occasionally photographers are tempted to improve a picture's composition by manually rearranging corals, rocks and other pieces of the bottom. Doing so can easily ________________ ______________________ and ____________ ______________________________________.

6. When you ______________________ you take at least three shots of the same subject, in which you vary the amount of light that reaches the film.

7. Silhouettes are among the few shots you are likely to take without ____________________________.

8. Close-up photos are generally those taken within _________________________ of the camera lens. Macro photos are usually taken ______________ ____.

9. Wide-angle photography makes everything look ____________________________. In the process, it can make murky water ______________________. Wide-angle lenses gather ______________________. This improves color saturation and allows us to shoot at __________________________________.

10. Repeating the same mistakes can be painful and expensive. Being able to avoid mistakes by referring to a __________________________ can save time and money.

How SSI's Total DiveLog System Works...

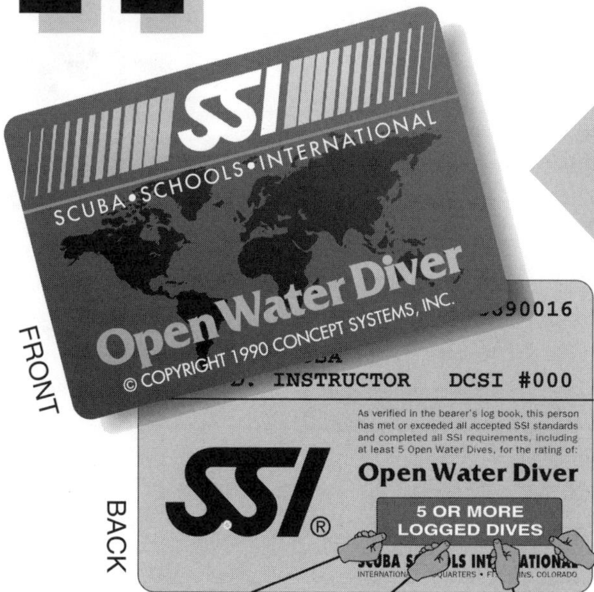

Level 1

LOG

5

TRAINING DIVES; GET THIS OPEN WATER DIVER C-CARD.

As you log more dives, you receive a sticker recognizing your achievement at each level!

12 OR MORE LOGGED DIVES

Level 2

LOG

12

TOTAL DIVES

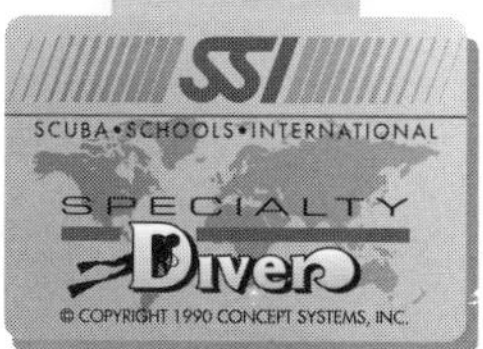

Include dives for 2 or more (total) SSI *Specialty Courses*

24 OR MORE LOGGED DIVES

Level 3

LOG

24

TOTAL DIVES

Include dives for 4 or more (total) SSI *Specialty Courses*

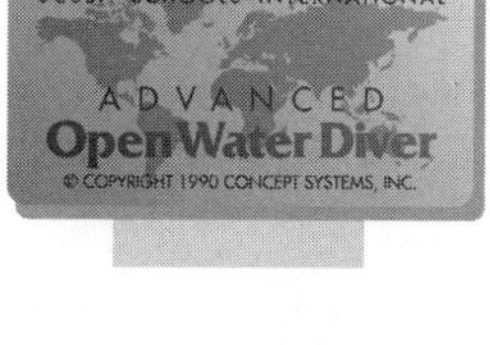

50 OR MORE LOGGED DIVES

Level 4

LOG

50

TOTAL DIVES

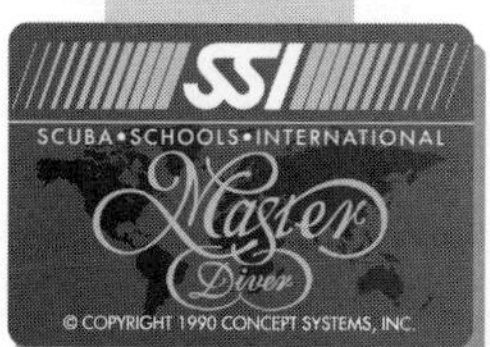

Include dives for SSI's *Diver Stress & Rescue Program* and 4 or more (total) SSI *Specialty Courses*

100 OR MORE LOGGED DIVES

Level 5

LOG

100

TOTAL DIVES

No extra training required; all you have to do to get this card is *apply!*

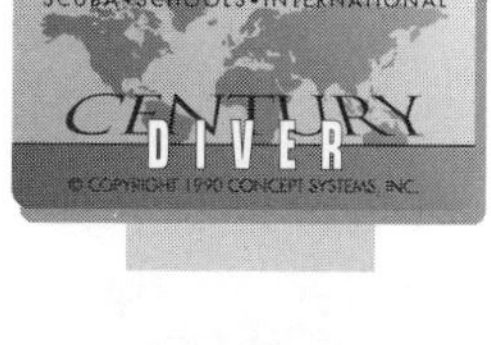

Notes

NOTES

Notes

Notes

Notes